ALCOHOL RECONSIDERED

Education for Moderation

Lesley Miller &
Catheryn Kell-Clarke

Guest Chapters
by
Sylvain Tiecoura

MAPLE
PUBLISHERS

Title: Alcohol Reconsidered
Sub-title: Education for Moderation
First published on Amazon 2021
Copyright © Lesley Miller, Catheryn Kell-Clarke and Sylvain Tiecoura (2021)

The right of Lesley Miller, Catheryn Kell-Clarke and Sylvain Tiecoura to be identified as the Author of the Work has been asserted by them in accordance with the Copyright, Designs and Patents Act 1988.

All rights reserved. No part of this publication may be reproduced, stored in a retrieval system, or transmitted, in any form or by any means without the prior written permission of the authors, nor be otherwise circulated in any form of binding or cover other than that in which it is published and without a similar condition being imposed on the subsequent purchaser.

A CIP catalogue record for this title is available from the British Library.

ISBN: 978-1-914366-20-8 (Paperback)
       978-1-914366-21-5 (eBook)

The authors of this book share their findings and opinions regarding the subject of alcohol. The authors of this book would strongly advice that you seek professional advice if you are struggling to control your drinking. The authors/publishers accept no liability with regard to this.

www.alcoholreconsidered.com

Published by:
    Maple Publishers
    1 Brunel Way,
    Slough,
    SL1 1FQ, UK
    www.maplepublishers.com

Book layout by:
    White Magic Studios
    www.whitemagicstudios.co.uk

For anyone who has ever questioned their drinking habits.

'This is a well-written book. It is personal, enquiring, and provocative without being sensationalist or self-pitying.'

~ Lucy Benyon, Journalist

Contents

Preface 5
Introduction 10
Lesley 14
What is Alcohol? 25
A Very Brief History of Alcohol 33
Cate 42
Tips for Moderating Your Drinking 59
Units and Measures of Alcohol 72
Sylvain 80
Alcohol and Your Body 89
Alcohol and Your Mind 98
Some History of Alcohol in the United Kingdom 106
The Marketing of Alcohol 115
The Impact of Alcohol 128
The Alcohol Problem 137
Is the Answer Prohibition? 140
Support Services and Treatments 149
Case Studies 157
Conclusion 165
Acknowledgements 171
References 172
About the Authors 185
Appendix 186
Further Help and Support 188
Index 189

Preface

Lesley

'Work is the curse of the drinking classes.'

~ Oscar Wilde

Like so many people, I had often fantasised about leaving my job to write a book. This, however, was never more than a fleeting thought, because as a primary school teacher and single mum, my work took up so much of my energy and commitment that there was never any time left at the end of the day to even begin contemplating putting pen to paper, or fingers to laptop.

Then 2020 happened. In January, I was signed off from my job with work-related stress. The new teaching position that I had started the previous year was not what it seemed. Without exaggeration, it was an absolute living hell and the thought of it, to this day, still makes me shudder.

I was under so much stress. I couldn't eat or sleep, and I constantly carried around a sense of apocalyptic, impending doom. I could have gone on long-term sick leave with full pay, but I knew that the situation wasn't going to improve. I didn't want to be a drain on the school's financial resources, and I really didn't feel that there was any resolution to the problem but to resign. So, with a very heavy heart, and an exceptionally anxious mind, I did just that.

Obviously, it was a very worrying and bleak time.

Several weeks later, things got a whole lot worse. The Covid-19 pandemic had arrived, and the world was turned upside down. At this point, I had no work, and the schools were closed indefinitely, so even supply teaching wasn't a possibility. My only option left was to apply for Universal Credit, a benefit we have here in the UK to support people while they are out of work. This wasn't what I'd call a proud moment after 20 years of teaching. It was very humiliating, in fact. I suppose the only comfort I had at the time was knowing that the whole world was in chaos too.

To claim Universal Credit, you need to be actively looking for a job, and I was assigned a work coach, Christina, to support me in my attempt to find employment. I won't lie, I was expecting Christina to be a bit judgemental of my situation, but thankfully, I was wrong. In fact, if it hadn't been for her unwavering support from the beginning, *Alcohol Reconsidered* probably wouldn't have happened at all.

When Christina asked me what I might do for work during one of our interviews, I told her the truth, and that was that I simply didn't know. Clutching at straws, I flippantly mentioned that I might set up my own business to support people who had problems with alcohol. This would, of course, all be based on my own experiences of drinking.

Christina really liked the idea. She told me that I could apply to join a business scheme through the Department for Work and Pensions (DWP), and that if the idea was approved, I would be assigned a business mentor to support me in becoming self-employed. After explaining the idea to Tola, my potential mentor, in what felt like a high intensity business pitch, *Alcohol Reconsidered* was approved.

This gave me some hope, and the excitement and relief of being granted such an opportunity during a time when things were so difficult was very motivating. I think that I knew from those initial conversations that I might have been on a very unexpected and different career path, which was a little unsettling because all I'd ever wanted to do, was be a teacher.

The concept behind *Alcohol Reconsidered* had been whimsically floating around in my mind for several years. It came about because historically,

I had what you might call, a drinking problem. By that, I mean I was drinking at least a bottle of wine every evening, often more. At the weekend I didn't even keep count. Some might call me an alcoholic. I also noticed that the amount I was drinking was steadily increasing as the years went by.

I had, like most people, attempted to moderate my drinking in several ways over the years, mostly in secret. I'm sure you can appreciate that, as both a teacher and a parent, I wasn't exactly wild about sharing this problem with my friends, colleagues or my doctor. There is still so much shame and stigma attached to drinking too much. I didn't know at that point just how common this issue was, and I had it pinned down as being some dreadful, inescapable character flaw of mine.

Sometimes I would switch to lager to reduce the number of drinks I was consuming, but I always ended back on the wine. Some weeks I would only allow myself to drink at weekends, but this never lasted long. A bad day at work would have me pouring a drink the minute I got home. There were untold attempts at abstaining, but with the exception of being pregnant with my son, I just couldn't make it stick for any length of time.

It wasn't uncommon for me to go for short stretches without drinking, but I'd still be thinking about drinking, or rather not drinking, constantly. It was just so draining. Despite all of this, all it would take at the end of a hard school day, was a colleague to say, 'Drink?' and I'd be there, throwing any resolve I might have had, out of the window.

My eventual, and it was eventual, route out of my drinking predicament was a better education and more realistic expectations of myself. The more research I did into alcohol, the easier it became to regain some control. Then, the more I knew, the less fear I had clouding my judgement. That's when it got easier to change my problem drinking.

I also learned there were scientific reasons behind why I liked, and still do like, a drink. I also began to understand that I didn't have to stop drinking completely in order to improve both my physical and mental health. This seemed like quite a revelation to me. I had assumed that my only option was to abstain forever, as that is the model we are presented with, if we find ourselves drinking too much for too long.

I knew that I couldn't stop drinking *forever* though. And besides, I wasn't at all sure I wanted to. Although I was fed up with drinking every day, I was, and still am convinced, that I really enjoy the social aspects of drinking. At the time of writing, the pubs are still closed in the UK and when I finally get into one, I can guarantee that I won't be ordering a diet cola.

I do wonder if the thought of being teetotal forever prevents many of us from even attempting to make any changes. In my own experience, I knew I couldn't go from a bottle and half of wine a night to complete abstinence. I wonder if we really have a good grasp of what moderation can mean on an individual level. We explore these ideas in the book.

When I shared my ambitions to write a book to accompany some training courses with Christina and Tola, I was really surprised at their enthusiasm. To have received such positive and unexpected feedback was really encouraging, and I was greatly appreciative of having something to distract me from the worry of the pandemic and how it was impacting our lives. To be honest, even I thought I was being wildly ambitious with what I was planning, but then I had another few more unexpected strokes of good luck.

The first was reconnecting, through social media, with Cate who I had taught with in London. She had decided that until the pandemic was under control, she would not be returning to the classroom either. I shared my *Alcohol Reconsidered* vision, and she kindly offered to help me finalise my business plan. At that point in time, I didn't know anything about Cate's drinking habits, or that she was going to eventually be the co-author of this book.

The second stroke of luck was making a connection on LinkedIn with Sylvain Tiecoura, an addiction practitioner, who works for the National Health Service here in the UK. He has extensive experience with helping people with alcohol issues. Sylvain took an interest in my vision for the business and offered to share his expertise. He is now a member of our advisory board and has written a few chapters for us.

The intention behind this book is to support you in evaluating and changing your relationship with alcohol in a way that isn't going to make you feel miserable or deprived. We're not going to pretend it's always going to be easy. At times it might be, but at others it probably won't. I would like us to guide you to make positive, and more importantly, lasting changes to your own drinking habits.

All our stories will share similarities and differences, but our reasons for drinking are complicated, as I believe our book illustrates. I very much hope that by sharing our research and thoughts we can together challenge some of the collective assumptions we have about alcohol. We hope to assure you that, depending on your circumstances, you won't need an 'all or nothing' approach. Change is possible and you don't necessarily need a sledgehammer to crack a nut.

Lesley

Lesley Miller & Catheryn Kell-Clarke

Introduction

Cate

'Here's to alcohol: the cause of and solution to, all of life's problems.'

~ Matt Groening (Homer Simpson)

Like Lesley, I have had a complicated relationship with alcohol. We chose 'Education for Moderation', as the subtitle of this book because for both of us, education and learning more about alcohol was the key to changing our drinking habits. Put simply, by educating ourselves more about it, we have been able to completely change our relationship with it. Now you might think this sounds just a bit too obvious coming from two ex-primary school teachers, but believe me when I say, it wasn't simple and there was nothing obvious about it. After both struggling with alcohol for most of our adult lives, it took educating ourselves about the booze; the history, the science behind it, the way it is sold and much more for us to really begin to understand the hold it had over us. All the subjects we thought we'd left behind in the classroom were actually very important in helping us to look more clearly at how and why we were drinking the way we were. By understanding more about alcohol, we came to realise that for us, it was possible to cut down our drinking rather than give it up altogether. We learned that we didn't need to feel guilty when we drank or slipped up once in a while as we were still gaining, just by cutting back, many of the benefits which go hand-in-hand with complete abstinence.

A word of caution, please don't think we've written this book purely for people who believe they are drinking at dangerous levels. You might be consuming one drink a day, or you could be drinking ten. We have written this book to support you while you are thinking about why you are drinking. In the same way that you don't have to be drinking above the recommended 'safe' levels to damage your health, you don't have to be drinking dangerous amounts to want to make a change to your relationship with alcohol.

Educating yourself about alcohol can only help you to make more informed choices. It's not necessarily about stopping, unless you decide that's what you in fact want to do. We hope that this book will be a resource that will signpost you to the help and support you are seeking. We can assure you that in this early stage of the book, there are many people feeling the same way as we did and you are right now. Problems with drinking are much more common than you might think.

The UK is certainly not the only country that has issues with alcohol consumption, which have become worse for some people due to the Covid-19 pandemic. By using our varied backgrounds, we are excited to be able to offer support to guide you to help change your relationship with alcohol.

We have focused on the aspects of alcohol that have interested us most because it is impossible to cover them all. Some of these topics we found very difficult to write about due to their personal nature, but at other times, were also very enlightening. We discuss the impact alcohol has on society and Sylvain shares information about support and treatment options that are available. We delve into the question of whether alcohol should be banned as we were intrigued by what we knew about attempts at prohibition in America and all that it entailed. We also share tips and ideas that have worked for us when cutting down our intake.

At no time, however, do Lesley and I want to portray ourselves as medical experts in the field of alcohol, though we are experienced educators. We are women who have reassessed and reconsidered our relationships with alcohol. We have been there, and done that, so to speak.

There are many different reasons why we drink too much and they are unique to each of us. Some of us drink because we enjoy it, some of us because we are psychologically or physically dependent on it. Many of us drink to deal with other health issues such as anxiety or depression. We will explore all these reasons and more in greater detail.

The three of us have our alcohol stories, which we will share. Whereas Lesley would often be wracked with guilt after her drinking sessions, I, on the other hand, could be called the fun drunk, the party girl, the one who was always up for a laugh during my drinking sessions. I wasn't really too concerned about the consequences and what the day after would bring. Sylvain has his own stories to share and has seen a wide range of alcohol related problems during his career.

This seems like a good place to briefly introduce ourselves a little more and to give you a snippet or two about each of us. We'll share more about our individual journeys in later chapters. As ex-primary teachers, with over 45 years' experience between us, Lesley has a considerable amount of leadership experience and holds the National Professional Qualification for Headship. This is something I never really aspired to as my passion revolved around the day-to-day classroom rather than that of leadership. I trained in New Zealand and taught there, as well as in Australia, Singapore, and England. I also have a background in the hospitality trade, so I know a few of the little tricks the breweries and drink producers use to entice us to drink. The Covid-19 pandemic was the final push which prompted both Lesley and me to take a break from the teaching profession.

Sylvain is the expert member of our team and he currently works with the NHS in Croydon. He has a history of working in healthcare and has many skills as well as insights into cognitive behavioural therapy, social services, group therapy, clinical research, and crisis intervention.

We also refer to a number of other experts in this book. The most prominently featured is Professor David Nutt. He is a world-renowned professor of neuropsychopharmacology, a medical doctor and psychiatrist, who has also been an advisor to the UK government.

Other experts are also referred to and we have compiled a list of their highly recommended books in the Appendix.

Lastly, I think it needs to be mentioned, the strange way we managed to put this book together. Due to the pandemic, we haven't actually met up in person. I have not seen Lesley for almost two years, and I have never met Sylvain in the flesh, but with the help of a sometimes reliable, and at times, not so much, internet connection, we have managed to write *Alcohol Reconsidered*. I'm in Hertfordshire, Lesley's in Middlesex and Sylvain is in Surrey. The wonders of technology, right?

We hope that you will find our book both interesting and informative and that it raises some questions worthy of your time and consideration. We want you to have, 'Wow, I didn't know that!' moments too. We've asked questions of you and we've tried to find the answers to some of ours. Saying that, we also hope that this book will leave you with more questions than answers and that it is a place to begin rather than a finishing point. It is fair to say that each chapter could have been a book in its own right, so we are really only scratching the surface. Our goal is that it will encourage you to do some of your own research and that will lead to questions that you may try to seek out the answers to.

Whatever your intentions are, and these may well change over time, we hope that we can help you develop your knowledge and understanding of alcohol. You may decide to read from beginning to end, or you may pick and choose the chapters that are of interest to you. If we can help you in even the slightest way, then we can rest happy that we have achieved our goal. Best wishes on your journey of reconsideration.

Cate

Lesley Miller & Catheryn Kell-Clarke

Lesley

'First you take a drink, then the drink takes a drink, then the drink takes you.'

~ F. Scott Fitzgerald

If you were hoping for a book about a reformed alcoholic who is now joyously teetotal, then you might be disappointed. I don't spend my evenings training to scale Kilimanjaro, nor do I spend my Sunday afternoons baking chocolate cakes, at least not yet. My story isn't *quite* as neat or as polished as that.

Changing my relationship with alcohol has been, and continues to be, a positive, ongoing process. There have been no quick fixes and there isn't any final destination that I'm trying to get to. I still have drinks with friends, I still have a drink most weekends, and I still spend a lot of time thinking about alcohol, though definitely not in the destructive way that I used to. I used to view not drinking as a real chore, a massive effort and that is probably because I had little idea about how good life could be without it playing a central role.

When Cate and I set about writing this book, we naturally talked about it with our friends, and some were kind enough to share their own thoughts and stories. Some of them were funny and some of them were very poignant. Alcohol is such an emotive subject, probably because of the amount of people who have either had their own problems with it, or their lives have been affected by it one way or another.

Your story might be similar or, it might be very different. And that is sort of the point. Our stories may, on the surface, share commonalities, but the reasons why we drink can vary enormously. The 'why do I drink?' question can be a complicated one.

Society still defines big drinkers as alcoholics, the ones who 'can't handle it', but the reality is, it's not so black and white. How much do you need to be drinking to be an alcoholic? You might read about my drinking and think that I didn't have that much of a problem at all, or you might read it and be truly horrified. I'm sure that what we can agree on is that learning more about alcohol can only be a good thing.

I would argue that anyone who claims it is easy to moderate or abstain from drinking has definitely not had a problem on the scale that I did. It hasn't always been easy exploring the 'whys', but equally, I wouldn't have called it a 'battle'. This word 'battle' is often associated with moderation and abstinence, and it doesn't really conjure up much enthusiasm for change.

By learning more about the reasons why people drink, which are quite complex, I began to understand how common this problem is. I really wish that I'd known that I wasn't the only one struggling years ago, because during my worst times, I felt very alone indeed. I wonder, if I'd known how widespread my problem was, would I have changed things sooner?

I also began to understand that my overwhelming enthusiasm for drinking wasn't necessarily all my fault as I had always presumed. There are scientific reasons why some of us become more reliant on alcohol than others, and we will explore these in greater depth.

This was important for me to know because prior to this, I had been berating myself for what I perceived to be a personal failure. I had never really considered alcohol to be an addictive substance and besides, we use that word 'addiction' all the time, but do we really know what it means? When I hear the word 'addict', I think about people who are out of control and beyond hope, not professional people drinking too much and too often. This, however, is often the reality.

Like so many others, my drinking had gone from being a fun, social pastime in my younger days to a daily habit, or even a ritual as I got older. It's difficult to pinpoint exactly when it became an issue as it happened very gradually over time, but I suspect it went from being fun with friends to something I began to rely on to cope with difficult emotions, probably in my late twenties.

Back then I was married to a musician, so life was, as you might imagine, one continuous party. There was always a gig to go to, even on a school night, and alcohol was just part of everyday life. It was also a lot easier to bounce back from a hangover. It was fun and I wasn't drinking any more than my peers, or so I told myself.

I certainly started drinking more when some serious problems occurred within my extended family, and around the same time it became clear that my relationship wasn't going to stand the test of time. I used to joke that Princess Diana was lucky when she said there were three people in her marriage, because there were about fifteen crowding ours. It just felt like over time that there wasn't really much substance to our relationship. I wanted to settle down and start a family. The partying was great, but it had started to feel a bit empty and shallow. The marriage didn't last, and at the time I was completely devastated. It felt like everything was falling apart. I felt like I'd failed.

I must have crossed the thin line from social drinking to something more noticeable around this time, because I remember overhearing my husband and his friend discussing my drinking. They were saying that they were a bit worried that I was drinking more than I used to, and I remember being absolutely furious with them for even daring to have this discussion. They weren't exactly light drinkers themselves, though I don't suppose at the time any of us had much of a clue about what a unit of alcohol was. I never mentioned what I'd heard but I was very resentful and worried that they were right.

As I moved into my thirties, I would crack open the wine the minute I got through the door from work around 6 pm. Teaching can be stressful, so there was always an excuse. I also noticed that over the years the amount I was drinking was steadily creeping up. It was getting increasingly easier to finish off a bottle of wine without feeling drunk, and I could often get a fair way through a second one.

Absolutely anything could be a trigger for pouring a drink. There was a wine for every situation possible, and it's a story you will likely have heard before. Of course, there were all the positive life events such as weddings, work successes and promotions. And then, alcohol was increasingly around for some of the more negative things that life threw at me; the bad days at work, the intense days, the uneventful days, and the disappointments. I am sure I drank as a way of coping with stress, anxiety and loneliness. Before I knew it, there was a drink everyday regardless of what sort of day it had been.

I wasn't the only one either. It is easy to justify and normalise your drinking habits when so many of your friends and colleagues are also drinking a lot. Big drinkers seem to have a radar for seeking out others who do the same, and it is reassuring to be surrounded by people who drink at the similar levels that you do. It normalises it. Naturally, we'd share the 'wine o clock' memes on social media and usually made a bit of a joke of it. It can't be that bad if everyone is doing it. That's what I used to tell myself.

It was about three or four years ago, or thereabouts, that I knew things really had to change. I distinctly remember sitting down one evening in floods of tears, feeling nothing but despair. I think it was because I'd given in to the temptation and bought myself a bottle of wine on the way home from work during some shot at abstinence. There wasn't a dramatic event like you see on the TV that meant I needed to stop. I was just worn down by it all. At this point I'd been drinking for so long that it wasn't unusual for me to get either dull aches or sharp stabbing pains in my sides, which were presumably caused by my drinking.

I was sick to death of the endless, endless drinking. By this time even thinking about my drinking had become exhausting. I was drained with the blackouts which happened at least once a week, and I was fed up with hiding the recycling. You know when you are taking mouthwash to work that you've got an issue.

People who drink a lot know how physically and mentally shattered you feel all the time. My days would begin by having to check my phone messages to see what conversations I'd had the night before and what arrangements I had made. And then of course, there was lugging around the self-loathing, the guilt and the shame. I was ashamed that I had no willpower whatsoever. I was ashamed that I wasn't being the best parent I could be. I was ashamed that this was the one area of my life I didn't appear to have any control over.

I'm not sure to this day to what extent people knew about my problem. Of course, those who loved and cared about me knew, but it wasn't something that was up for discussion. It was just how it was, and I expect those who know me best had just learned to accept this over the years. I suspect that it didn't come up at work because I was reliable and very capable at my job. There was never a time I missed work because of my drinking, and I'd always been very dedicated and committed to my career and pupils.

The only person who was brave enough to even mention the issue was my mum. If, and when, she expressed any concern, she could look forward to me reacting quite explosively. I wouldn't have put this down to any sort of denial on my part. I just couldn't bear the thought of discussing it. Once she sent me a text message alluding to the idea that my drinking meant that I probably wouldn't see my son making it to adulthood. I rewarded her for this concern by sending a venomous reply and not speaking to her for days. If you have a problem with alcohol, it's probable that you are all too very aware of it, and you do not appreciate anybody pointing this out, especially not your mother.

I think most addictions can make people unintentionally quite selfish, and I was no different. I didn't like my mum pointing out my flaw one little bit, but I never really looked at it from her point of view. It was convenient for me to forget that my Nana, my mum's mum, had died from cirrhosis of the liver through drinking. At times I felt like I was being punished for judging Nana's drinking so harshly when I was young. It must have been awful for mum worrying about me and the impact this might be having on my young son.

We will explore later in the book the relationship between alcohol and our mental health but as you can see, it wasn't helping mine. It makes me feel sad when I think back about how all this drinking has affected my self-confidence over the years. I'd say I'm a relatively confident person, but at times I've found it difficult acknowledging my successes relating to work, or parenting, or anything else for that matter. It's difficult to see yourself in a positive light when the only thing you focus on are your faults.

Even as I write this, I'm nervous about the reaction of others, and there's a lingering dread knowing that my family and friends are going to be reading this. I did speak to my sister, Leanne, about my decision to reveal my past drinking problems, and I asked her if she was worried that I might be causing embarrassment to the family. Her reaction was that she was proud that I'd done something about it, and laughed at some of my ridiculous drunken antics of years gone by.

As you might expect, one of the questions I've asked myself is when did this all really begin, and have I had a problem with alcohol right from when I took my first drink?

My drinking career began when I was a teenager back in the nineties. Back then, once you were 13 or 14 you were given more responsibility and babysitting was your main source of income. It wasn't, unfortunately, anywhere near as lucrative as it is today. Often, along with our £5 wages for the evening, there were usually a few cans of lager thrown in for good measure. We didn't feel too hard done by. In fact, we were quite happy with this arrangement. Every Saturday night I would be left with two cans of Heineken and access to anything I wanted to eat from the fridge. If memory serves me well, microwavable French bread pizzas were all the rage, but I digress.

I can remember drinking the lager, with its vile, bitter taste and wondering how anybody could enjoy it. That didn't stop me from trying though. We'd been told at school during our science lessons that alcohol wasn't physically addictive. Of course, doctors and scientists know so much more about alcohol now than they did back then. This might explain why what some of us think we know about alcohol today is outdated.

Underage drinking was relatively easy in the nineties. We were forever infuriating local pub owners by going in for our first legal pint, only to watch it dawn on them that we had been frequenting their establishment for at least two years beforehand. Asking for proof of age wasn't as enforced as it is nowadays. According to the Institute for Alcohol Studies, research shows that younger generations are in fact the ones who are drinking the least these days, but back then, that wasn't the case. We were the drinkers and we were proud of it.

In my case, I'd been very studious at school, and the chance to be rebellious provided me with a great opportunity to show off. I suppose I foolishly wanted to prove that I wasn't just a swot, as I'd always been mercilessly teased about at secondary school. Though I've always been outgoing and didn't need a drink to deal with shyness as was the case with Cate, I did want to fit in with the crowd, as teenagers do.

Alcohol Reconsidered

My female friends and I were quite proud of ourselves on the drinking equality front too, insisting that we would be drinking pints of lager and not halves, as was thought acceptable for women at the time. Drinking was a feminist issue. We enjoyed the kudos we received from our male friends for being such enthusiastic drinkers, and I'm certain that this egged us on even further.

One friend, Amanda, who was both beautiful and clever was a sight to behold when we went out. We used to work at Woolworths together as Saturday girls on the music counter, the height of cool back then, and after work we would go for a drink. Not only could she drink the men under the table, but she was a brilliant pool shark. Amanda would challenge the men to a pool tournament and completely wipe the floor with them, all with a pint in her hand. We were all impressed with her ability to challenge the norms of the day and to prove that women could do anything men could do, including drink.

Naturally, our parents were not anywhere near as enthusiastic about our drinking as we were. Well, mine definitely weren't. My mum doesn't drink at all unless you count a very rare Pina Colada. The only time that I ever saw my dad even remotely tipsy as a child was once a year, when he went for one or two drinks for his work's Christmas 'do'. My siblings and I were always excited about this event as we would be given all of Dad's loose change upon his return. A pound back then was big money, so all of his coins were the equivalent of a lottery win for us.

My Dad also had some very fixed ideas about drinking, probably as a result of his strict Yorkshire upbringing. It wasn't considered 'lady like' back then for women to drink pints of lager. I remember a time when we had a bit of a friendly argument in the pub one day. He asked me what I wanted to drink, and I asked for a pint of lager. My dad's response to this was that he was happy to buy me two half pints, but he wouldn't buy me a lager in a pint glass. I can't recall who won the argument, but

I suspect that being quite the stubborn feminist I eventually wore him into submission, if not then, certainly over the years.

As we came of age at 18, many of us worked in pubs and bars. When I was at university, binge drinking was very much expected of you. It was the era of 'Cool Britannia'. We'd spend Saturday afternoons playing drinking games with the intention of getting drunk, which seems somewhat ironic when you consider how many of us are now spending our lives trying *not* to get drunk.

I imagine many of us continued to enjoy the social aspects of drinking as we established ourselves in our careers and continued drinking into adulthood.

I suspect that my generation was lured into the drinking world in the first place by the alcopops of the day. Five pounds was all we needed for a night out, which was a good job because that is about all we had. Remember the babysitting money? This amount back then would buy you a Castaway, which basically tasted like pineapple, and a Diamond White, which was a 'cool' bottled cider. We would combine them in a pint glass to make what we referred to back then as a 'Blast-Away'. One of these, as the name suggests, was enough to get us very drunk indeed. This was before I'd built up any tolerance or needed to drink more to achieve the same effects.

The alcohol industry spends incredible amounts of money effectively marketing alcohol to us from the minute we are old enough to drink, and it is quite literally everywhere we turn. We find it in supermarkets, on social media, television and in films. Nobody starts out drinking with the intention of developing a drinking problem, but you can see why if you're having so much fun, you'd want to carry on. Cate looks more deeply into the marketing of alcohol.

I do sometimes wonder if the fear of failure keeps so many people locked into drinking. I was afraid of all the words I'd started associating with it.

The media uses the terms 'alcoholic', 'dependence', and 'addiction' in relation to heavy drinkers, and I'm not sure how helpful they are. They all sort of imply that the drinker should be blamed, that they are being irresponsible. Like I said, I have plenty of friends and colleagues who are big drinkers too, but they don't identify as being alcoholics.

Perhaps another barrier that prevented me from changing my drinking sooner was the fact that I'd been drinking for so long, if I took the drinking out of my life, what would I find and what would I do instead? I wasn't sure how I would fill my time and I wasn't sure how I'd cope with life's difficulties. Like many people who stop drinking there was the worry of the 'boring' label, which was a bit of a cheek because I'm sure the world could have managed without me dancing on tables, and I'm sure I haven't been dazzling anyone over the years with my drunken repartee. I suppose the health and wellbeing brigade's reputation for being a bit 'holier than thou' also put me off changing my ways.

Learning about what alcohol is from a historic and scientific point of view and just how prevalent a substance it has been in nearly every civilisation also played a significant role in changing my perception towards it. In the past, I hated alcohol and the impact it was having on my life but ironically, it was by learning about how alcohol works and the social benefits of drinking, either perceived or otherwise, that helped me to untangle my complex and jumbled thoughts.

It's always inspiring to read about people who have managed to turn their lives around, and I like to read the stories about people who used to drink to staggering levels and now don't touch a drop. I love reading about how much more they are enjoying their lives and what they are achieving. If you have ever given up for a bit, you will know the benefits that moderation or abstinence can bring. When I first drafted this chapter, I made a list of all the benefits I felt from not drinking as much, but I concluded that it was patronising. Just like the route you take moving forward is personal to you, so too are the benefits.

For me, one of the greatest things is having a positive relationship with alcohol again. It doesn't feel like it's dragging me down anymore. I'm happy to have a drink at home at the weekend or if something genuinely exciting or awful happens. If I'm ever tempted to drink for the sake of it, I'm usually able to analyse why and make more positive choices. That might be playing the guitar or gardening, or any number of other things that I would previously have regarded as being boring or a bit self-indulgent.

I hope that this chapter will have set the scene so to speak and given some context to the book and why we wrote it. In later chapters, Cate and Sylvain will introduce themselves and tell you their alcohol stories. Alcohol is a complex drug, and I really believe that it is worth exploring in more depth. I doubt I'm ever going to abstain completely, but I don't really see that as my main goal now. For now, I want to continue to enjoy all the social aspects of drinking, but with less damage to my health.

I think it's important to know how this drug manages to keep a hold over so many of us, and know what we can do about it if we do run into trouble.

What is Alcohol?

Lesley

'Not all chemicals are bad. Without chemicals like Hydrogen and Oxygen, there would be no way to make water, a vital ingredient in beer.'

~ Dave Barry

In preparation for writing this chapter, I asked some of my friends what they knew about alcohol. Most of them associated drinking with socialising and relaxing, as you might expect. Their understanding of the science, though, could be described as somewhat vague at best.

My point here was not to prove that my friends are stupid, obviously. I did this to confirm what I suspected, that our understanding of alcohol is somewhat limited. Our knowledge tends to derive from our own personal experiences, rather than from experts in the field or up-to-date research.

The science

The word alcohol is of Arabic origin. It is 'al gawl' which means 'the evil spirit' or 'the thing that gives wine its headiness'. Pronunciations and spelling do and have changed across space and time.

Ethanol, or C_2H_5OH, is the alcohol we drink and is different from the other forms that are used for fuels, medicines and cosmetics. These probably wouldn't taste that great and would likely cause you some considerable harm if you consumed them. Alcohol is obtained through the processes of fermentation or distillation. This chemical is the baseline ingredient that is present in various proportions in the many different beverages that are available on the market.

Is alcohol a 'proper' drug?

We use the word 'drugs' all the time, but do we really know what they are or how they work?

The definition of a drug is, *'...any natural or artificially made chemical that is taken for pleasure, to improve someone's performance of an activity, or because a person cannot stop using it'.* (1)

Most of the friends that I questioned knew that alcohol was classified as a drug. But when I questioned them further and asked whether they actually thought of it as a drug, the answer was a resounding 'no', or at least not in the same way that we think of drugs such as heroin or cocaine. This came as no surprise when you consider the fact that alcohol is both legal and generally considered socially acceptable.

I have often wondered why alcohol is permitted by law and other drugs are not. Is it because the sale of alcohol brings in so much revenue to the treasury that the economy would collapse if the government banished it or perhaps because there would be riots if they did? Previous attempts at prohibition across the globe have had varying degrees of success.

Socially acceptable

So why is alcohol a socially acceptable drug and others are not? Perhaps the answer lies with how long it has been around, and the role it has played in almost every culture since civilization began. Interestingly, during both the Victorian and Edwardian periods, people drank alcohol for health reasons and not so long ago, doctors used alcohol to treat both physiological and psychological illnesses. We now know that drinking too much can actually cause anxiety and depression. It's a bit like smoking cigarettes which was also recommended by doctors in the past. (2)

Are drugs the road to ruin?

I'm not sure about you but I was brought up to know that if I headed down the path of drug addiction, my life would be ruined, and I would more than likely die. That is how dramatic and clear cut the messaging was, both, from my parents and the television. This was illustrated brilliantly by the hard-hitting storyline on the BBC children's show, Grange Hill. This was very popular in the UK whilst I was growing up in the 'eighties. One of the show's much-loved characters, Zammo McGuire, developed a heroin addiction and we were all horrified by this.

We all got the message loud and clear back then, 'Just Say No!' Drugs were to be avoided at all costs, so it does seem strange that we had, and still have, such a relaxed attitude towards alcohol. If I asked you to think of a drug addict, I expect that you would be more likely to conjure up visions of gangs and social deviants living on the outskirts of society rather than middle-aged people pouring themselves a few drinks every evening.

But alcohol is a drug just like any other and its potential to do damage is just as great.

Professor David Nutt, who used to be the UK government chief drugs advisor, made clear back in 2009 that alcohol was in fact, the most harmful drug in the UK. This followed some of the most sophisticated and detailed analysis that had ever been conducted. The findings were based on how widely it was used and not necessarily the harm it caused individuals. Interestingly, at this point, alcohol wasn't even allowed to be considered as a drug by the UK Advisory Council on the Misuse of Drugs. This, despite scientists knowing for a fact that it was. This, for reasons that you and I can only speculate about, did not come as welcome news and Professor Nutt was very unceremoniously sacked. (3)

What type of drug is alcohol?

There are quite a few different categories of drugs and they affect us all in different ways. Firstly, there are the **stimulants**, or 'uppers' if you like. These are drugs such as cocaine, nicotine and caffeine and their appeal is that they have the capacity to increase your attention and focus, and give you more energy in the short-term. **Depressants**, or 'downers', such as benzodiazepines and GHB are drugs that can relax and calm you down. Then there are the **hallucinogens**, such as LSD which may make you feel detached from reality and can alter your perceptions, thoughts and emotions.

Opioids and **opiates** are another class of drug. Examples of these are morphine and heroin, which in the short-term may make people feel very relaxed or high. The difference between these two is that opioids are synthetically created in a factory and opiates are naturally occurring, in poppies. And finally, we have **Novel Psychoactive Substances (NPS)**, which are legal highs and were designed to replicate the effects of illegal substances like cannabis, cocaine and ecstasy. (4)

Where does alcohol fit in?

Alcohol is complicated. **It is a psychoactive drug.** These substances work by altering our mental processes such as our perceptions, our levels of consciousness, cognition, and our moods. Initially, alcohol acts as a stimulant, and we drink for the effects that it produces, such as lowering our inhibitions, making us more self-confident and sociable or perhaps to help us relax. In the short term, this works. That is why we like it.

Medically speaking, however, alcohol is classed as a depressant. That doesn't mean that it makes you depressed, although it can over time. It means the more of it you drink, the slower your brain function and neural activity will become. This is just a more technical way of describing what you and I know about being drunk. It is common when we have had a few too many to slur our speech, and bang into things due to our poor coordination. I expect you will be aware of random bruising after a big night out. Alcohol delays our reaction times, and it causes us to make poor decisions. If we drink enough, it can make us black out or even kill us.

How does alcohol work?

Alcohol works very quickly and so after five to ten minutes of you having a sip of your favourite tipple, it begins taking effect. Around a fifth of the alcohol that you consume is absorbed through your stomach lining and the rest passes into your bloodstream through your small intestine. The alcohol stays in your bloodstream until your liver breaks it down which it does at an approximate **rate of one unit per hour**. This depends on a range of circumstances such as how healthy you are, whether you are eating or have eaten before you started drinking, whether you are male or female, or even your ethnicity. Until the liver breaks the alcohol down and gets rid of it, you can find yourself both physically and mentally impaired.

Neurotransmitters

Have you ever woken up and wondered why you did something so stupid the night before? Of course, you have! This sort of behaviour can be explained by science. Essentially, this is a result of how alcohol affects two neurotransmitters in our brains. The first one of them is called **gamma-aminobutyric acid** or **GABA** for short. Put simply, GABA blocks certain brain signals and decreases activity in your nervous system. You might say that it can produce a calming effect. The other neurotransmitter, **glutamate**, does the opposite. These two are a team and they work together and I, very unscientifically, like to think of them as a set of weighing scales that need to stay in balance. If you have too much Glutamate you can become anxious, have a seizure, or end up with brain damage. If you have too much GABA, it stops you from forming memories, you may make real lapses of judgement or at worst, you could stop breathing.

Neuromodulators

Alcohol also affects different neuromodulators. **Neuromodulators** are your body's chemical messages, and you may have heard of these because they aren't just affected by alcohol consumption. The first one is **serotonin** which is a mood enhancer and can make us more empathetic. It can also make other people seem more attractive, so if you've ever made an unorthodox romantic choice under the influence, you can probably put this down to the serotonin.

The second of these neuromodulators is **dopamine** or dihydroxyphenethylamine. Easy to write down, but difficult to say. Dopamine can be thought of as the brain's reward system and when you drink alcohol, your brain gets a hit of it. We like dopamine, and this is also the reason why we can get addicted to virtually anything, not just alcohol. Dopamine is responsible for our motivation, our drive and our energy. It is thought that the effect alcohol has on dopamine is more significant for men than women, which may explain why men are still more likely to be heavier drinkers than women.

Lastly, we have **endorphins**. Endorphins are linked to feelings of pleasure, reward, and pain reduction. Research in 2012, led by Jennifer Mitchell, a clinical project director at the Gallo Centre and Adjunct Assistant Professor of Neurology at the University of California San Francisco, found that when we drink alcohol, our brains release endorphins. Interestingly, the research also found that the heavy drinkers in the study reported greater feelings of intoxication than the more moderate drinkers. This study found that the brains of heavy drinkers are changed in a way that makes them more likely to find alcohol pleasant. Perhaps this is a clue as to how problem drinking develops in the first place. (5)

We can see then that we appear to get some pleasure from those initial drinks, but another big problem is that alcohol also switches off the frontal cortex of the brain which is responsible for control. This explains why some of us find it hard to stop at one or two.

What is addiction?

People can become either physically or psychologically addicted to alcohol, and it's easy to see why. We start drinking because we like the short-term effects, then as our bodies grow accustomed to it, our tolerance increases, and we need to drink more to achieve the same effects. If you continue to do something to the point of harming yourself and just can't seem to stop, this would be classed as an addiction. (6)

Not everybody becomes physically dependent on alcohol, but if you've developed your tolerance, and then start seeking it out more often, you can see why this can start becoming a problem. Our brains are wired to remember the pleasure we get with drinking.

In today's world, you could argue that the word 'addiction' is overused. Is there anything we can't be addicted to? I personally don't particularly like some of the words associated with problem drinking. Abuse. Misuse. Dependency. They all seem to imply that there is no hope for you, that there is no way back, which just isn't true. I also wonder if they make us feel like we are being wilfully irresponsible, rather than people who need some help and support.

Why do some people get addicted to alcohol and not others?

There isn't one single reason why people get addicted to alcohol and it can affect anybody regardless of their sex, socio-economic status or ethnic background. That said, some research suggests that men are twice as likely to develop an alcohol problem than women. (7) This makes me question if this is not just down to differences in physiology, but how some men spend their leisure time.

A genetic risk

Some studies in America and Europe suggest that between 45 and 65 per cent of our propensity to addiction is down to genetic factors, though there isn't an alcoholism gene as such. Your fate isn't sealed if you have alcoholic parents, but it might be something to think about. (8) What role did alcohol play in the lives of those you grew up with? I wonder if more people knew that genetics play a role in alcohol dependency, the problem might not be so taboo?

Other factors

Alongside your genetics, there are also social and environmental factors to consider. Those of us who start drinking at an early age, are more likely to end up with addiction issues. If you grew up in poverty, or with poor family relationships then you are also more likely to run into trouble, as are those of us who face 'peer pressure', have experienced trauma or who suffer from mental health issues. All these factors can put you more at risk.

How do we know all this? Well apparently, a lot of testing has been done on rats. Researchers found that bored rats in an unstimulating environment are more likely to 'self-medicate' and drink alcohol than rats who can socialise, have sex and groom. I think that will resonate with many of us as we've spent much of the last year in some form or another of lockdown. (9)

So, we can conclude that we know that alcohol is a drug that affects each of us in different ways. Genetics, social and environmental factors can all contribute to the risk of us developing an alcohol problem. I would argue that far more needs to be done to educate us about how alcohol works, and the medical and social impact it can have on us. Access to information like this would inevitably allow us to make more informed choices. The question we might ask ourselves is, how can this be achieved?

Alcohol Reconsidered

A Very Brief History of Alcohol

Lesley

'No thing more excellent nor valuable than wine, was ever granted by the gods to man.'

~ Plato

We tend to think that problem drinking is a very modern phenomenon, when in fact, it goes back a lot longer than you might think, probably to the dawn of civilization and at the very least, since records began.

Prehistoric man

During my research, I stumbled across an article about the work of Robert Dudley, a physiologist from the University of California and the author of *The Drunken Monkey: Why We Drink and Abuse Alcohol*, which was published in 2014. (1) According to Dudley, it might be helpful to consider alcohol addiction from an evolutionary perspective, and he suggests that humans may have an intrinsic drive towards drink. I'm not sure about you, but if I can blame my drinking patterns on prehistoric man, I'm definitely going to.

Dudley hypothesises that back when we were primates, between 18 and 45 million years ago, alcohol was beneficial in calorific terms. Primates developed the flavour for alcohol and evolved to smell the naturally fermenting fruit on the forest floors. They weren't drinking 13 per cent bottles of Merlot obviously; it would have been much, much weaker. Dudley certainly isn't, however, suggesting that prehistoric man was eating this rotting fruit with the aim of getting drunk. It makes sense though, given that alcohol has a high calorific content that it would, when food was scarce, have been an invaluable source of energy. Perhaps this may have been the reason we came down from the trees in the first place.

Dudley also suggests that our modern-day fondness for alcohol might be, if you will excuse the pun, some sort of evolutionary hangover. Alcohol, fats, and sugar are far more readily available nowadays than they used to be. So maybe we just haven't evolved fast enough?

The latest research suggests that younger generations are more likely to binge when they do drink. However, they appear to be drinking less than other generations. (2) Perhaps we are, as a species, beginning to evolve, or perhaps the youth of today have seen their parents behave so disgracefully that they've decided to give it a miss. The jury is still out on that one.

Incidentally, it has also been found that when male fruit flies are rejected by a potential suitor, they gravitate more readily to a high alcohol containing fruit. I'm sure that most of us can relate to that. Apparently, it would appear, there are a lot of similarities between humans and fruit flies. (3)

Ancient civilization

If we want to develop our knowledge and understanding of alcohol in its entirety, perhaps it would be helpful to look at how much of a prevalent role it has taken in nearly every culture and society you can think of. Most cultures have an alcohol story, and it appears that it was present throughout ancient civilisations. Name any nation and the use of alcohol, or its prohibition, has been part of its story. This includes cultures and places we don't often associate with drinking, such as the Middle East. That is, unless you were raised as a Christian, in which case, you may remember that Jesus' first miracle was turning water into wine.

I discovered that the first drink of beer would have been very unlike what we are used to drinking today. We know from chemical tests that beer dates back to around 3500 BC, which is so far back in time that it is beyond my imagination. It might go back even further than that, possibly as far back as 10000 BC. There is some evidence that workers were paid with beer in Iraq during this time. Archaeologists think that beer making may have played a key role in the very beginning of civilization and there is evidence of strong links between alcohol and agriculture. (4)

Ancient China

It is believed that the Chinese were the first civilisation to make wine in around 6000 to 7000 BC. The wine was made from grapes, hawthorn berries, honey and rice so one can only imagine what this may have tasted like. I'm almost tempted to have a go at making it. How do we know this? Back in 1983 archaeologists discovered wine residue in pottery jars and drinking vessels in the Shaanxi province. (5) Apparently in ancient China they used to drink the wine warm with flavoured additives. It was viewed as a sort of spiritual food and was often consumed when offering sacrifices to the gods.

Just as today, the Ancient Chinese drank alcohol for pretty much every occasion; to celebrate, to commiserate, before going into battle, to celebrate a birth, or a battle victory, or when someone passed away, at weddings as well as for inspiration. So, the same reasons as us really. We also know that alcohol brought a lot of money into the treasury, just as it does today.

Although the Chinese liked to drink, they also recognised that it could be dangerous. There were 41 laws against making wine. There were several emperors who 'liked a drink', and it wasn't unusual for citizens to be buried with some alcohol to make sure they could still have a tipple in the afterlife. (6)

A commentator from 650 BC said:

'...people will not do without beer. To prohibit it and secure total abstinence from it is beyond the power of even sages. Hence, therefore we have warnings on the abuse of it.' (7)

The 'drink responsibly' message is not a new one then.

Ancient Egypt

If you said 'Ancient Egypt' to me, I would naturally think of Tutankhamun, pyramids, hieroglyphs, black eyeliner and that sort of thing. I'd conjure up images of scantily clad, sweaty men lugging around slabs of heavy rock under the sweltering sun, parched and dehydrated. It appears however that the Egyptians were a lot more joyous and laid-back than I'd imagined. There's a decidedly good chance that they could have drank both you and me under the table.

If you are worried about your drinking, take comfort in the fact that you might have nothing on the Ancient Egyptians who did not drink moderately at all. In fact, they drank to get completely out of their minds. We tend to take a dim view of excessive drinking and promiscuity today, but in Ancient Egypt, they were all for it - the drinking and the sex. What you or I might consider today as problem drinking was the exact level of inebriation the Egyptians aspired to. Getting legless wasn't just socially acceptable, it was expected of you. In fact, they thought that moderation was something to be sniffed at. Sober shaming, it would seem, isn't anything new either. (8)

The Egyptians had a lot of gods connected with beer and wine. They believed that the whole of humanity had been saved *because* of beer.

The story goes that Ra, the most important god of all in those times, got really fed up with mortals behaving so selfishly, so he decided to teach men a lesson, as gods often do. He turned the Goddess Hathor into a Sekmet, a lioness, to destroy them. Sekmet would rip people limb from limb and enthusiastically drink their blood with gusto. This carried on for quite a while but then the other gods pointed out to Ra that, if this continued, there wouldn't be anybody left to teach a lesson to. So, he thought about it and had a change of heart. Ra got a red concoction of beer together and deliberately put it in Sekmet's way. Sekmet thought this was the blood of humans, so naturally drank it and got very, very drunk until she passed out. When she awoke from this drunken stupor, presumably with a big headache, she had turned back into Hathor. Humanity had been saved. Hurrah!

The Egyptians had a festival to commemorate Hathor and it was called 'The Festival of Drunkenness'. Brilliant, isn't it? By all accounts, it was as good as it sounds, and the Egyptians would drink to the point of passing out. They believed that getting roaring drunk would bring them closer to the gods, a spiritual experience if you like. There are reports that there would be a lot of sex at this festival too, orgies even. (9)

Not surprisingly, you didn't have a very long lifespan if you were an Ancient Egyptian. Those who survived childhood had a life expectancy of around 30 years if they were female and 34 years if they were a male. Given their astounding enthusiasm for drinking, one has to wonder if it was their pickled livers that killed them and not the diseases around at the time.

So, what were they getting drunk on exactly? The beverages available back then were beer or wine. Only wine was very expensive, so unless you were wealthy, you would drink beer. And it wasn't just the men who drank a lot either. The women of Ancient Egypt were also very enthusiastic about drinking and were more than welcome to join in the fun and frivolity. (10) Not all ancient cultures, however, were as liberal and ahead of their times as the Ancient Egyptians, though. Take the Ancient Greeks, for instance.

Ancient Greece

Unlike the Egyptians, the Ancient Greeks were somewhat more considered, but they still had a complicated relationship with alcohol. Well, the men did. Women were not allowed to drink at all. It's confusing trying to work out their exact take on drinking. The Ancient Greeks were wine drinkers, but they had drinking rules. They would water down their wine and generally tried not to overdo it, as drunkenness was seen as a lack of discipline. The Ancient Greeks spent a lot of time *thinking* about drinking as they did everything else, and they held regular drinking parties, known as symposiums.

Symposiums were only attended by men. Unfortunately, if you were a woman in Ancient Greece, you didn't have much status. Women were certainly not invited to symposiums, well not unless they were providing the entertainment in the form of dancing, flute playing, prostitution or possibly a combination of the three. A symposium started with a basic meal which wasn't accompanied by wine. After they had finished eating, they would have their hands washed by slaves, the perfumes would be sprayed and the floors swept. They would lie about on pillowed couches to have deep conversations whilst drinking wine.

The evening would start with one of these men being elected as the symposiarch, and he was basically the boss for the event. He decided what wine the men were to drink, how much they were going to drink and what they were going to talk about. He also decided whether it was going to be a moderate evening or a heavy drinking session. The men were expected to drink at the same pace as the symposiarch. The wine was dished out and when one krater, which is an ancient Greek vessel, was finished, another one would be ordered. (11)

Eubulus, who was a fourth-century comic poet and Athenian statesman had this to say:

'For sensible men, I prepare only three kraters: One for health (which they drink first), the second for love and pleasure, the third for sleep. After the third one is drained, wise men go home. The fourth krater is not mine anymore - it belongs to bad behaviour; the fifth is for shouting; the sixth is for rudeness and insults; the seventh is for fights; the eighth is for breaking the furniture; the ninth is for depression; the tenth is for madness and unconsciousness.'

~ Ebulas: The Fragments (12)

He probably said this because despite the best of intentions, you and I both know what happens when you try to drink but not get too drunk. Sometimes you are lucky and it works, but more often than not, it doesn't. And it was the same for the Ancient Greeks. Apparently, they would often end up doing some sort of conga down the street, causing chaos and mayhem as they went.

The Roman Empire

The early Romans were a bit like the Greeks when it came to alcohol. They were a bit uptight about it. They too watered down their wine as drunkenness was frowned upon, if you were a man that is. If women were caught drinking, they could face the death penalty. Men would even kiss their sisters, to see if they could smell alcohol on their breath and catch them out.

Still, once the Roman Empire started bringing in the money, attitudes towards alcohol seemed to relax a bit. Men were drinking more and they were eventually kind enough to let the womenfolk partake. Naturally, the more money you had, the more access you had to the most expensive alcohol. But all was not lost if you were a bit lowlier. If you were aiming to get fed and watered well, you had to be part of a banquet system called a convivium. If you were poor and you wanted to get an invite to one of these banquets, which were held quite regularly, you just had to hang around looking good and flatter the egos of the wealthy. You weren't by all accounts treated with much dignity at these events, however, but you did get your hands on some wine. You had to know your place in Ancient Rome. (13)

The Roman Empire had it good for about 1000 years but then, for a number of complicated reasons, it all went wrong. This leads us on to what was happening around this time closer to home.

The Dark Ages

After the collapse of the Roman Empire, Europe was thrown into what we know as the Dark Ages. Back then in Britain, if you were poor, you were more likely to be a beer or an ale drinker than a wine drinker. The commoners in the Dark Ages would have had a staple diet of ale, as it was more of a food substance than a drink. It was ale for breakfast, ale for lunch, ale for dinner and ale for supper. Apparently, they were putting away about a gallon of it, per person, per day. That is a substantial amount even by our standards. (14)

It seems strange to us nowadays to consider that alcohol might historically have been better for us to drink than water, but it's probably true. Mark Forsyth (2017), explains in his book *A Short History of Drunkenness*, that we might have started farming around 9000 BC, not to produce food as you might expect, but to start making alcohol. He goes on to suggest that beer would have been easier to make than bread, and more nutritious as it contained vitamin B. The alcohol would have also killed off any harmful parasites and bacteria. It might be said that the beer of yesteryear would have been better for you than the beer of today, and it certainly would have been much less intoxicating. Nevertheless, they were still drinking rather a lot of it.

Alcohol Reconsidered

Evidence suggests that beer was used as payment for work throughout several civilizations, which does actually make sense, to me at least. I have to confess that I did think in my younger years that my employers should just send my wages straight to the pub and be done with it.

It was around these times that monasteries became heavily involved in brewing, and the monks made wine both for religious and personal use. The average monk had a daily allowance of three gallons. When you consider that there are five bottles of wine in a gallon, that's an incredibly generous personal quota of 15 bottles of wine *a day*. It comes then as no surprise that the Anglo-Norman bishop, John of Salisbury (1176-1180), had this to say:

'The English are noted among foreigners for their persistent drinking.' (15)

We in the UK are still regarded as particularly heavy drinkers. It's a reputation that we just haven't been able to shake off, although if you care to look into it, we're not actually the worst in the world, or even Europe for that matter.

So, there we have it. We've always known, perhaps with the exception of the Ancient Egyptians, that alcohol has its advantages and its perils. It has been used in religious festivals and ceremonies from as far back as we go. Even today, wine represents the blood of Christ in Christianity and all religions have a stand on it, whether they permit it or not. Ancient history seems to show that the stance on alcohol by leaders throughout the ages has remained similar overall. You're allowed to drink, just not too much. It's interesting to think that nearly every society and civilization has had the same problems with alcohol that we have today.

Lesley Miller & Catheryn Kell-Clarke

Cate

'I cook with wine, sometimes I even add it to the food.'

~ WC Fields

My alcohol story also has many bumps and bends, probably just like yours. Like Lesley, I don't want to stop drinking. I do, however, want to be more aware and thoughtful about my choices when I am having a drink. Reconsidering these choices and developing a deeper understanding of alcohol has helped me to become both happier and healthier. I've learnt over the years that guilt is just such a waste of time and that it does no one any good. Yes, I've been a bloody idiot at times, but every day is a new one, a fresh start and feeling guilty about the past is not an option. If I fancy something to drink, then I'll have it. More often than not, I won't. I have found other things to fill the gap that alcohol had occupied for so long.

Talking with Lesley whilst writing this book showed me that some of the issues we were all having around alcohol were similar. As corny as it may sound, I was looking for some kind of guidance or at least the feeling of support that someone had been in my shoes and understood the situation.

Now to my drinking stories, how are they any different to Lesley's? My neighbours? Workmates? Or yours for that matter? Well, they're not, really. All alcohol stories tend to be similar. Sure, the characters are different as is the setting, the plot, the triggers, the alcohol and generally the ending, but essentially, they are all the same. The excitement, and the joy that drinking first brings and then, the all-too-often despair or the cringe-worthy moments that can follow a big night out.

As a dumpy, little redheaded kid growing up not too far from the bottom of New Zealand, I was probably about eight or nine when I had my first taste of alcohol. My dad was a hardworking sheep farmer, and he really loved a beer in the evening, a Speights, which was a local brew. He would often give me a sip. I loved the fizz and the gorgeous golden colour of the beer.

He's not been around for many years now, but I know he wouldn't mind me saying this. In the past, my dad liked a drink and as a young man, along with other young farmers in the district, used to, by all accounts, get up to all sorts of mayhem. I have no real recollection of how much he drank but after he died in 1991, Mum would often share with me some of the more hair-raising stories about him. He frequently drank beer, but he was known to have the occasional whiskey too. The whiskey was often won at various bowling tournaments. You see, my dad was a great bowler, both indoor and lawn, and winning prizes seemed easy for him. Alcohol made an easy prize. Back in the fifties and sixties drink-driving didn't appear to have been such a big issue either, certainly not in New Zealand. The cars were, back then, built like tanks and the country roads in New Zealand were quiet and there weren't too many police around. The young farmers, by all accounts, thought they were invincible.

Mum, the ex-primary school teacher and now the farmer's wife would have a rare special occasion gin and tonic. Looking back, I wonder if she drank infrequently because of her standing in the community. As a teacher and member of the local church, maybe she had more of an image to uphold. To be known as a drinker, wouldn't have really fitted with that stereotype. In fact, around the world, I wonder if it's more common for males to be seen as the drinkers in a family. It seems to me that men's drinking is shrugged off and viewed as normal, whereas with women it is, I believe, more often frowned upon, even now. Think about the different ways male and female characters are portrayed when they are shown to be drinking on TV shows or in movies. The men tend to be portrayed as suave and sophisticated while the women are often depicted as loud and a bit brash.

When I was 15, we moved into the nearby small town which felt like a metropolis to me. It was the kind of place where farmers could generally get whatever they needed for their sheep farms, where their wives could get the supermarket shop done, and the kids could get new school shoes, a haircut or the occasional ice cream treat. Every weekend, the local sports teams would compete and then retire to either their clubhouse or one of the two pubs. It was, to my young eyes, big but upon reflection, it was a small country town just like any other.

It was here things changed dramatically for me. I suddenly had a social life, something that had been very limited whilst living on the farm. I joined the local theatre group and became entrenched in its dramatics, both on and off the stage. I joined the tennis, basketball and netball clubs, and I was, at long last, able to hang out with my friends outside of school hours. Now alcohol, it seemed, played a significant role for many people of this town where there wasn't, I'll be honest, a great deal to do. As I said, the local drama society became a huge part of my life. There were drinks after the rehearsals, the opening night parties, and closing night parties. More drinks after a show, and bus trips to the theatre in the nearest city. We would drink on the bus there and back. Gosh, there were even parties to reminisce about the parties.

This shy farm girl had developed a taste for alcohol, any kind really, but most often whiskey and cola, beer, and occasionally, a little wine. Fizzy and sweet from 'exotic' Italy, most likely. I loved the buzz and my apparent loss of shyness that came with the drinking. I could, and still can be, quite dramatic with a drink or two inside me. I'm sure over the years people have noticed the change in my demeanour when I'm having a drink. I can go from quiet Cate hanging back or in the shadows, to party Cate after the first few glasses of fizz. I became known as 'CKC Just One More'.

Alcohol Reconsidered

Alcohol was often seen as a rite of passage back home, just as it is in many countries and while underage drinking is discouraged, and obviously illegal, it is something that happened and continues to do so with frightening regularity. The legal drinking age in New Zealand, like the UK, is 18, but kids as young as 15 or 16 were often able to obtain alcohol and drink, under the watchful eyes of the supposedly more sensible adults.

I left high school with just enough qualifications for university, as parties were so much more fun than study and exams. Uni was a real eye-opener to life with cheap alcohol, partying and, of course, surviving on my own. Drinking sessions were very frequent with the odd lecture or tutorial thrown in. I loved student life but unfortunately, my exam results weren't great, and my parents were less than happy about the time and money they felt I was wasting. I can still hear dad saying, *'Why don't you get a job and earn some money of your own?'* So, that's what I did. I dropped out after two years and went into a hard but high paying job in a shearing shed, as a wool-handler, picking up after the shearers and sorting the shorn fleeces. I saved hard to travel and after nine months, I flew on a one-way ticket to London. I was off on my big O.E. or overseas experience, a very Kiwi thing to do.

London had always held a very special place in my heart, especially the theatres, the landscape, and the history. The Royal Academy of Dramatic Art intrigued me, and I had a hankering to attend auditions and tread the boards of the West End. Big dreams, right? I landed in England with a rather big bump, a little lost and a lot alone. Eager to find my way in the world, within a week, I'd managed to find a room in a flat in Hackney and a job in the West End, at a pub just behind the Ritz, off Piccadilly. Pretty fancy, for the farm kid from New Zealand.

It was here that I became very aware of the enormous alcohol choices that were available. The pubs back home often served only one brand of gin, whiskey and vodka and perhaps two or three beers. This was such an exciting time for me. I experimented with all kinds of alcohol and I felt very grown-up, sophisticated and popular. The uniqueness of a 20-year-old Kiwi on her travels during the 'eighties was novel, especially in the posh West End. The alcohol gave me the confidence to speak more to the customers. Not drinking on the job, of course, but once my shifts had finished, I was drinking with the regulars. This was, I felt, a way to quickly integrate myself into London life. As a side note, a few drinks also helped me to understand the English accents better. I could comprehend more easily what the people were actually saying. When I first met my husband, Martin, I couldn't make out a word this lad from Newcastle, a Geordie, was saying. A couple of drinks in me, and all that changed.

I worked in that pub for a year, but the auditions proved trickier than I had ever imagined and so I moved on, to a fabulous wine bar on the outskirts of the City of London. This bar catered mainly to wealthy businessmen. It closed at 9 pm, which gave the 'suits' and me a good couple of hours' drinking time at the nearby pubs. I now tended to drink what the lads drank; gin and tonics, and lots of them. Scarily, I could keep up with them and still get home in one piece. I didn't give my drinking a second thought nor that of my safety or what I was doing to my health. I always made it home safely, and thankfully lived to tell the tale. I would be back ready for work at 10 am the following morning. Lucky? An idiot? Perhaps I was both.

After two and a half years, my working visa was well and truly up, and I returned to New Zealand with more than I was planning. Excess luggage, you might say. I was pregnant! Mum was immediately supportive when I told her my news. Dad, however, took quite a while to come around to the idea, six months, in fact. It wasn't until he saw his first granddaughter, then only a few hours old, that he spoke to me again. Her father, Martin, was not on the scene, or even in the same country for that matter. We'd lost contact after I moved from the West

End and we'd meet up with mutual friends for drinks and a catch-up every six months or so.

I was, as they say in New Zealand, a solo mum on the DPB, the Domestic Purposes Benefit. (1) Not a very enviable position to be in. Thankfully, I now had a very supportive family and I made the decision to return to university the following year. Baby under my arm, and books in my backpack, I decided to follow in both my grandmother and mother's footsteps and I began to train as a primary school teacher. Once again, alcohol was always present. This time I was hanging out with the other solo mums who were also studying and mad enough to be at Uni. They were always up for a drink and a natter. My baby was cared for in the university creche and I would be at the pub.

Studying and single motherhood was really tough. I had a very small support network and these ladies offered me a life-line in a world that I was very new to. Mum was over an hour down the road and I had no mother-in-law or any other family to help out.

To cut a long story short, Martin managed to reconnect with me through our mutual friends and he came out to New Zealand to visit. There was more drinking as I showed him the sights. When he drunkenly asked about my daughter's father, I bluntly told him the truth. He was shocked, to say the least. Surprised and nervous to meet his new daughter, he was happy nonetheless, and after my graduation we joined him in the UK to live as one new, happy family.

Back in the UK, my first job was at Victoria Wines, a posh bottle shop chain, that is sadly no longer around. Oh, how I loved my little job. The pay was rubbish but the excitement of the different wines that were on offer quickly made up for that. Wine tasting sessions on Saturdays, wine club on Thursdays and recommendations to the rich customers. I was in my element.

But like I said, the pay was dismal and after Martin and I married, I made the call to return to the classroom. I took on supply teaching with gusto. Travel to the schools, which were frequently in London's East End was a two-hour journey, give or take, both ways. Thankfully, a refreshing drink was always waiting at the end of the day. The village where we lived had around 12,000 people and was blessed with more than 13 pubs. You know, the old-style traditional ones with worn rugs on the uneven wooden floors, open fires and stag heads hung on the walls. The ones where even I needed to duck down to get through the doors. So many pubs to choose from and again, so many alcohol choices. I loved the village life. However, as a new family, buying a house in the UK was never going to be a real option. House prices in the county were well above the UK average and so we were on the move again. Back to New Zealand, Auckland this time.

I've taught my way around the world and have absolutely loved everywhere we have lived. We lived in Auckland for four years. After Auckland, we were in Sydney for eight years, and then up to Singapore. We spent 10 years there, and then finally we returned back to my beloved UK. The pair of us just don't seem to have strong settling down genes.

In all of these countries, alcohol was never far from my mind. Was my drinking a problem? Or did I just think it was? I honestly wasn't sure. Some days, usually when I was nursing a hangover, I worried about my love of drinking. On other days, I was the first up to the bar to get the next round in.

There was a time in Singapore, when my best friend and I ran the after-school drinks, where we both worked. The cheap alcohol flowed and the shenanigans that frequently followed were a regular Friday night feature. I was like a duck to water. I continued my love affair with alcohol and the drink loved me too, or so I thought. My husband has a great switch which turns on when he gets drunk and ninety per cent of the time it activates his homing pigeon mode, usually resulting in me being dragged along as well. But left to my own devices at after-work drinks, it's a different story. Not just one or two and then off home for me. No, I was, again, that last woman standing, often swaying to the music. It also helped that I was the woman selling and serving the booze.

Again, it was the loss of my shyness that the drinks brought to the table that I particularly enjoyed. Being a teacher and talking to at least 25 kids at once is one thing. Having a conversation with another adult, in a social situation, without alcohol, for me was something entirely different, difficult and nerve-wracking. Essentially, I am a shy introvert. This may explain my attraction to the theatre, the make-up and costumes that I could hide behind. Having said that, depending on the situation, when you first meet me, you may think I am anything but retiring.

I don't recall too many terrible mornings after, pull-the-duvet-back-up-over-my-head mortifying moments. As mentioned, I see myself as more of a fun-loving party drunk, the one who's up for a laugh rather than that person who is willing to share their deepest, darkest secrets with anyone who will listen. Nor am I that drinker who can become mouthy and insulting or embarrassing to their mates. I was never really one for leaping into fast-moving cars. I'd more than likely be the one asking loudly for just one more from the DJ who was about to close down for the night or blagging my way through the backdoor of the nightclub with my mates and talking our way out of the cover charge because there was only three hours' dancing time left.

I do remember once at the annual Beerfest in Singapore, we'd treated ourselves and bought the V.V.I.P the very, very important person wrist bands which essentially allowed us continuous amounts of alcohol for a very good price, $100 from memory. Somehow, we were ushered into the V.I.P section, not the V.V.I.P section. Needless to say, I was less than impressed and already with a skinful of booze, I told the usher so. Someone in the V.I.P section took offence and I somehow ended up with a pint of beer being poured over my head. Not one to take this lying down, I retaliated with the nearest thing to hand, a plate of hot chips and sauce, which was deposited all over the offender's white, and probably very expensive, T-shirt. This caused it all to kick off. The whole of the V.I.P section erupted. My mates joined in the ruckus that ensued. Beer and food flew! Chaos! Needless to say, we were all promptly kicked out of the wrong section and escorted out of the Beerfest, tails between our legs. Me drenched in beer and covered in food, my mates in varying degrees of disarray. Looking back, it's all a bit hazy and a very silly, and possibly dangerous situation. Something I would never have dreamed of doing without any Dutch Courage inside me.

Many more crazy alcohol-fuelled fun and games ensued, but after ten years in Singapore, both Martin and I agreed that a change was due. We were sitting in a local English-style pub one very stormy Sunday when we decided the idea of running a pub ourselves should become a reality. The time felt right. Research had shown us that the English tenancy process made this the most realistic way that we could make this happen and running a village pub had been a long-held desire for us. There's something about the pubs in the UK, they are so different to those in any of the other countries I've lived in. Pubs in New Zealand and Australia tend to be large barn-like spaces and somewhat impersonal. In Singapore, they were often poor versions of an English or Irish one and just not on par with the originals. I quite fancied myself as a Kiwi version of Bet Lynch, from Coronation Street or perhaps an East Enders Peggy Mitchell. What were we thinking? Many of our mates thought we were completely bonkers. Looking back, they were, it seems, entirely correct.

You're probably thinking right now that perhaps me running a pub was not a particularly sensible idea. I'm the first to admit I've done some pretty stupid things when I've been under the influence. Yes, I have danced on tables and jumped naked into a freezing garden pond. Don't ask! I've also lost more than one mobile phone and just like Lesley, I have woken up in the morning after a big night needing to read through my phone messages to remind me again of exactly what I'd done. Perhaps at the back of my mind, I had the idea that running a pub would allow me to drink and still be in the safety of my own home? Who knows? I really didn't.

And so, we moved back to England, with our two Singaporean cats and signed up for a lovely old pub. It was smack bang in the middle of a gorgeous little market town in the Cotswolds complete with friendly locals and more importantly, lots of lovely rich tourists.

Reality quickly set in and it became apparent that running a village pub was not all what it was cracked up to be. There's more to pulling a few pints and chatting all day to your customers. We knew it was going to be hard work but neither of us had ever imagined how much of an impact it would have on our personal lives. Easy access to alcohol and living on-site resulted in us both developing a habit of expecting a few drinks after a day's hard work, just like everyone else. Except for us, this was happening at around midnight and it quickly became a regular habit of one or two pints, perhaps followed by a wine or two. Sparkling wine was always my first drink of choice as the wine bottle stoppers were notoriously unreliable. It made sense for me to drink the lot. That half-empty bottle of prosecco would be flat by tomorrow and we couldn't possibly sell fizz-less fizz.

Being behind a bar again did, however, give me a very good insight into how alcohol can impact people's lives; both the good, the bad and at times, the ugly. We had the regulars who were frequently propping up our bar at midday, nursing the first of their many daily pints. We saw the sadness that often went with solo drinking. We both watched as couples matched each other drink for drink. One would be drinking large glasses of Chardonnay while the other, on much weaker pints of ale. We witnessed too the inevitable arguments and frequent tears that would almost certainly follow.

Of course, we were also privy to the celebrations and fun that we so often associate with alcohol too; the births, the engagements, the birthdays, and the wakes. Saying 'no' when someone offered to buy us a drink wasn't an option and while we had made it a rule to never drink when we were on duty, we kept a record and saved them up, for after closing or our next night off. My nights off were either spent drinking with the customers or more likely, upstairs in the flat, pyjamas on, catching up on the latest movie, with a bottle of fizzy wine close at hand.

We had many great times and Martin and I both agree, we would not swap the experience for the world but after 18 months, we were both jaded and tired of the lifestyle. We agreed we had gone as far as we could with the pub, and so I decided to go back into the classroom and Martin back into IT.

We moved again, back down to London. What's the first thing you do when you move into a new neighbourhood? You look for a good pub or wine bar. Living in West Kensington, we were spoilt for choice. Excellent public transport also meant there was very little need for a car so no danger of being behind the wheel and over the limit. Perfect. I worked at various schools as a supply teacher. Most were great, some not so much. A relaxing bottle or more after a hard day in front of someone's little angels once again became my norm.

After a few months, I landed a role at the school where Lesley worked. She was in the next classroom. We hit it off immediately and remained friends after we both left the school the following year. Funnily enough, Lesley and I were not at the pub together a great deal. Where we worked, wasn't very close to any pubs so after school drinking with colleagues was a bit of a rarity, more a special occasion, for the end of term or birthdays or the like.

After leaving the school at the end of the year and to try and save some money, Martin and I moved again, out of London into another little market town with, yes, you guessed it, plenty of pubs.

Do you see a pattern?

Living in Hertfordshire was fabulous but those continually itchy feet resulted in us making a decision to return to Sydney. The beaches, the sunshine, a better teacher's salary, the wine, the beer, and the fact that our daughter still lived there. A one-way ticket was purchased, and I flew off to Australia in the middle of January 2020, to begin teaching at the start of the Australian school year. Martin and our now old cats were to follow me, mid-year when all loose ends in the UK had been tied up. On paper, this all sounds like a great plan, right? Wrong!

Much catching-up on old haunts and favourite wines followed, and after reacquainting myself with our daughter, her friends, and the delights of Sydney, I began work at the end of January at a little primary school in the city. A very good friend was the principal there and I was to be teaching my most favourite subject, drama, to the whole school. I was so happy to be back in Sydney and life was pretty good, or so we thought.

Can you see what's coming? We couldn't, nor could most of the world. Covid-19 had begun to grab the news headlines in early 2020, as you all know. Mum also became very unwell around this time and so I made the decision to make a quick trip to New Zealand in early March to visit her. I stayed with her for two weeks where she appeared to be improving. Upon my return, the first lockdown in Australia began. My initial two weeks of self-isolation quickly turned into two months and put paid to any thoughts of returning to the classroom. This was heartbreaking. I had only just begun to get to know the children and the staff and I was missing them all terribly. I felt so lonely and miserable. The excitement of living in a new place in a new city meant that boredom wasn't an issue, there were still places to explore on my walks and there was planning to be done for when Martin and the cats joined me mid-year.

My relationship with alcohol, however, changed dramatically at this time and I was often drinking at least one, sometimes two bottles of wine from a large glass every day in front of the constantly updating news. The fun Cate had gone and was quickly replaced by a new scared Cate. I was terrified of the virus and I drank to try and blot out what was happening around me, alone in Sydney. The media in Australia was relentless with TV, radio and papers all reporting on the pandemic.

The pandemic forced me to brutally weigh up my health options. I have Type 1 diabetes and over the years, it was something I had never given a second thought to. There was never really any need as it was well-controlled, and I was healthy. The pandemic suddenly meant I had a giant target plastered on my back. Sadly, diabetics made up a large number of the many deaths worldwide. Type 2 or late-onset diabetes is generally caused by lifestyle choices and these diabetics are often overweight. Type 1 diabetics usually present with the disease when they are children. I was an anomaly as I was diagnosed with Type 1 when I was 30 years old and weighed eight stone. Having diabetes didn't mean that I was more likely to catch Covid-19. If I did, however, it could cause me to have more severe symptoms and complications. I was absolutely petrified. (2)

Our plans of making a new life all too quickly turned to custard. Because of the pandemic, the Australian government changed the visa rules and Martin couldn't obtain one without waiting a considerable amount of time, fourteen months or so. The cats couldn't be shipped either and so they would not be joining me. I was alone. So much stress and such a lot of lonely solo drinking followed. I'd always been a glass half-full kind of girl until the pandemic and then every glass became very empty. The glass was broken. There was nothing in it but despair, self-pity and isolation.

Despite the fact that our daughter lived only three miles away, the lockdown meant we couldn't visit each other. Quite frankly, I may as well have still been in the UK. Essentially, I spent the time alone and terrified. What did I do? I think you probably know the answer. I drank and drank and drank as I tried to numb the horror of what was going on in the world. The local wine delivery company was on speed dial and wine was delivered, by the case, with concerning regularity. My life was rapidly spiralling out of control.

Martin and I decided that I should try to return to the UK pronto as my sanity, physical and mental health, and finances were very much at stake. I managed, thankfully, to obtain an exclusion pass and flew back to the UK at the end of May. A lot more drinking followed. For all the travelling I've done in my lifetime, flying has always been terrifying for me. From my first flight in 1984 to the UK, I have never lost my fear of flying, no matter how many times I do it. That sense of having absolutely no control over what is happening. Needless to say, I have always taken advantage of the free drinks offered onboard. It was such a relief to be back, yet at the same time so terrifying. The UK had a huge number of deaths and cases compared to other countries.

Some more Covid-safe drinking, and sitting tight with hubby in Hertfordshire ensued. We were desperately trying to enjoy the English summer with both eyes and ears fixed on the frightening daily news. Covid-19 was not going away from Europe, at least anytime soon.

When I arrived back in the UK, I had every intention of returning to the classroom and I reached out to my previous teaching supply company and was welcomed back with open arms. It became apparent, however, that my returning to the classroom in the new school year wasn't a safe option for me. This was truly disappointing, as I loved teaching, but I trusted it wasn't forever, my positive pants were on, and I knew it was the right decision. I couldn't risk contracting the virus and so I started looking into different possibilities.

Living on a single wage hasn't been easy but, like so many others in 2020, we've managed. I'm happier, and safer, staying at home, hanging with Martin and the cats. I've been reading and writing, instead of being in a classroom with children and all of the potential risks.

Mum's health continued to deteriorate and it was distressing watching her unable to answer questions or perhaps even recognise us. Maybe she could hear us as I spoke to her on Zoom, I don't know. I'll never know. It was heart-breaking being unable to touch her or to soothe her fears. Talking is one thing. Holding someone is another. The complete feeling of helplessness, being on the other side of the world as mum lay confused in her bed in the nursing home was awful.

Mum died at the end of August and I had no way of returning easily for the funeral. We watched it, heartbroken via a one-way live feed at, due to the time differences, midnight, with a very much justified large drink in hand. I wish I'd had the chance to say goodbye and attend her funeral, to mourn her loss with my relations. I still haven't seen her grave. I don't know when I will. Maybe this year. Maybe the next? I don't know. The thing that has kept me going is the belief that she and dad are now back together. Really tough times.

This might sound harsh, but I'm glad mum died in August, when I was back in the UK with Martin for moral support. This, I admit, purely from a selfish point of view, because had she died when I was alone in lockdown in Sydney, I think that would have been a serious tipping point in my mental health. Mum's death, however, did result in Lesley reaching out to offer her sympathies. They were greatly appreciated. We reconnected, and the rest, as they say, is history.

Alcohol Reconsidered

It was also around this time that I came to the realisation that, while I wasn't an alcoholic, my drinking was a cause of concern. However, it was time to pull up those positive pants again and get on with it. The glass needed to be full, not half full. I needed to be positive.

Now you might be wondering how Martin feels about my drinking. I know he wasn't particularly fond of the nights I'd stumble in from a Friday session in Singapore. However, he can give as good as he gets. He's a Geordie after all. Drinking is also in his genetic make-up. I love him with all my heart and he is the love of my life, but there are times when he would challenge me about my drinking and I hated him with a passion. He now understands and I think he is proud of me as I am reconsidering my alcohol choices. Martin certainly enjoys a drink, goodness, remember we met in the pub behind the Ritz, but he generally has more willpower and knows when and how to stop. While he'd never stop me from having a drink, I knew deep-down that he wasn't really happy with the way I behaved when I drank too much.

With the UK lockdown, the pubs closed and me not around, Martin had reduced his alcohol intake to almost zero. Rather than drinking, he'd found other things to occupy his time such as TV box sets and movies. When I arrived back, he suggested we try Dry July, a month without alcohol, which I agreed to. I won't lie, it wasn't easy. Our local supermarket must have felt a loss when our weekly delivery order amount dropped dramatically as I replaced the beer and wines with the cheaper low or no alcohol options. Water, squash, and some pretty dreadful alcohol-free red wines were now to be found in our shopping. Some of the non-alcoholic beers proved popular as they taste like the real thing and they have continued to be a regular purchase.

You could say the pandemic was a massive turning point for me. By developing even more understandings about alcohol and discussing my choices, it has helped me see that I can be pretty cool sober. Yes, I still love a cold beer on a hot day, the few we had over summer, or a glass or three of delicious red but I'm more conscious (pun intended) when I am drinking. I used to sit, watching the TV, glass always in hand.

I'll still have a real beer or a glass of fizz, just not as often. Maybe we'll share a bottle of wine with a meal perhaps once a week, maybe every two weeks. There are no set rules now. While in the past I'd be reaching for the bottle because it's Friday. If I fancy a glass of Chardonnay with the curry I've just made, then we'll have a glass. I am more in control and can choose whether I drink or not. I think about drinking as more of an occasion now; nice glasses, finer wine, candles. You get the idea. Perhaps as time goes on and alcohol-free wines will improve, I'll give up completely. I don't know at this point. I'm happy where I am at the moment and I now understand that it doesn't have to be an all or nothing choice. Some alcohol in your life can be beneficial as we will discuss.

Well, that's me in a nutshell. So, what brings you here? What piqued your interest? Have you tried to stop drinking and feel that you've failed? Or are you just beginning on the path of rediscovery? Are you reconsidering your options? You've decided to read this book so that's a great start. There are a huge number of support organisations and apps that can also assist you should you choose to use them. Maybe you want to try things on your own. That's cool too. We did. We believe it's about educating yourself about what alcohol is and does. It may get a bit bumpy but *Alcohol Reconsidered* might just be able to offer you some support to make the bumps just a little less jarring and painful. Good luck with your journey.

Tips for Moderating Your Drinking

Cate & Lesley

'Drink moderately, for drunkenness neither keeps a secret, nor observes a promise.'

~ Miguel de Cervantes

Lesley and I have both found over the years of reading self-help books, that they tend to have the help or 'how to' section at the end. When we were deciding on the order of the chapters, we thought it made more sense to include some ideas and tips for moderating early on in the piece to give you longer to mull things over as you are reading the rest of the book. While we are convinced that education for moderation is the way to go, cutting down or abstaining is something that needs support early on, and the ideas in this chapter might just give you some sort of inspiration on your journey. The purpose of this book, after all, is to help you reconsider your options, to make better choices and in doing so, to feel healthier.

We know from our own experience that different approaches work. What is working for Lesley is finding out more about the science and history of alcohol and in making ongoing, achievable changes. For me, it was understanding more about what alcohol does to your body and also the long history behind it. What works for you, or somebody else reading this book, will more than likely be something different again. This is why a number of self-help books, although useful in some ways, didn't resonate with us entirely. Many of the authors had found their route out of drinking and seemed to assume that we should all copy them, following what they did. Whereas we believe the type of action you decide to take will depend on your own reasons for drinking and how risky it has become.

What you will find is that these ideas can be broken down into the following areas:

- Wanting to do it and reading this book is a great start
- Having a plan to help you achieve your goals
- Using tips, tricks & tools to help you stay on track

It's your choice

For some people, complete abstinence may be the best option to take, while others can learn to moderate. Whichever option you decide to go for, and this may change over time as you have a bit of practice under your belt, it's going to take some self-awareness. This is, in our opinion, easier to do if you reflect on how alcohol works and you challenge some of your thoughts. We'll share some of the strategies that worked for us, but again, you might well find your own depending on what it is that you are ultimately trying to achieve.

Before you start moderating your drinking, there are a few points we believe you need to consider.

Know your why

It is a cliché, but you really do need to know your 'why'. (1) Now, it's likely that you have more than one reason for reconsidering your relationship with alcohol but try and concentrate on the one that means the most. It is tricky but try to stay focused. My reason was health, and the fact that I want to live to old age despite having diabetes. Lesley's motivating factor was also her health, both physical and mental. Yours might be money or your relationships or something completely different.

The right mindset

Another thing to stress is that we honestly believe that you need to be in the right place to start this process. Adopting an 'I can' mindset is very important and only you will know whether or not now is a good time to begin making changes. If you're currently drinking to help you cope with a difficult life event, it's probably going to be more challenging, not impossible, but more challenging, at least initially. Try using positive language. You might need to reframe your thoughts from 'I can't have a drink.' to 'I can have a drink if I want to. I'm just choosing not to have one at this point.' Remember, nobody is forcing you to do anything and that it is your choice. A lot of people run into trouble when they are trying to make changes to appease someone else rather than themselves.

If you go out, intend to have a good time no matter what your drink of choice is, rather than going out to drink and *then* having a good time. Sure, there will be mitigating circumstances, but I'm sure you'll find the whole experience to be a lot more satisfying and therefore, more achievable.

If you've been feeling guilty about your drinking, we hope to assure you that you really shouldn't. People drinking alcohol for its mood-altering effects are, as you know, something that has been a part of the human experience for literally thousands of years. Lesley touched on this in the chapter, 'What is Alcohol?' Remember Dudley's Drunken Monkey theory? When used properly, alcohol can enhance milestone experiences, enables us to connect with strangers, helps people to really relax and enjoy the moment, and creates an atmosphere where new ideas and connections naturally occur.

Conduct a review of your drinking

It is important to be honest with yourself and know how much and why you are really drinking. We often underestimate how much we drink whether knowingly or unwittingly. A simple way to start this process is to create a list or chart to help you assess the positives and negatives of either cutting back or continuing to drink. Perhaps you could rank these reasons in order of importance. You might need to keep revisiting this and save it somewhere prominent for motivation. (2)

Reasons for reducing your drinking - the positives

Do you want to improve your health, maybe lose some weight and get fitter? Or perhaps save a few pennies? It could be something like wanting to avoid hangovers and potentially serious health problems in later life. It could be more complicated such as wanting to improve your relationships and work more productively. It could also be none of these reasons and something entirely unique to you.

Reasons for not reducing your drinking - the negatives

What are some of the reasons you may have for not wanting to reconsider the amount you are drinking? Are you worried about how your friends may react if you give up? Or is there the fear of missing out or do you feel more at ease when you have a glass in your hand? Perhaps you're worried that you won't be able to relax without a drink? Again, everyone has their own reasons and there are many. (3)

Preparation

Once you have some ideas on why you drink, you can now decide what you want to do, and work on getting a plan together to help you. This is very important and there are a number of things you can do in preparation for reducing your alcohol intake.

SMART drinking goals

> *'A goal without a plan is just a wish.'*
>
> ~ Antoine de Saint-Exupéry

One of the things that has really worked for us is looking closely at the weeks ahead and decide what and when we'd be drinking. We did this by setting SMART goals.

You've possibly heard of them and they can be as complicated or as simple as you want to make them.

SMART is an acronym for specific, measurable, achievable, relevant and timely. Let's break that down even further.

Specific or what exactly are you hoping to achieve with regards to your drinking? What are you hoping to accomplish? This could be viewed as the mission statement and you need to consider the 'W' questions: Who? What? When? Where? Which? Why? when thinking about this.

Measurable or how will you know when you have achieved your goal? Set some milestones and think about specific things or tasks you hope to accomplish.

Achievable or how important is changing your relationship with alcohol to you? What do you need to do to achieve this goal? Do you have the toolbox or support or skills you need? If not, how can you get them?

Relevant or why are you setting this goal?

Timely or how long do you intend to give yourself. Remember it takes time to rewire your brain and reset your thinking. Set a realistic timeframe to make the changes but remember not to be too lenient on yourself either. Without realistic timing, it's very likely that you are not going to succeed.

Some possible goals could be:

- I only want to drink at weekends for the next month
- I'm only going to drink when I'm eating with friends

- I want to be able to drink at parties and other events without getting drunk (4, 5)

Consider what is realistic for you and how long you will give yourself to achieve your goal. A week? A month? This might be linked to how much you drink and how often. For example, if you are used to drinking every night, you might start by introducing a couple of alcohol-free days a week or you could reduce the number of drinks you are consuming each day and week. Try to identify the times that are going to be most difficult for you. Times such as that between the end of the work day and dinner, or after dinner and before bed. Or maybe your challenge will be, attending social events? (6)

Small changes will help to build up your confidence. Perhaps you could have your first drink later in the day? Maybe you could choose to drink something with a lower strength, in a medium glass rather than a large one, for instance?

Count & measure

You'll need to consider how you are going to track your progress. Are you going to measure the number of drinks per day or in units? Skipping ahead to the chapter on units and measures might be helpful.

Perhaps you could create a table, make marks on a calendar, or keep notes on your phone. Recording each drink before you consume it can help you slow down. (7)

Knowing standard drink sizes is important too so you can count your drinks more accurately. Depending on what country you are in, these vary. You could measure your drinks at home, rather than just guessing. It can be hard to keep track when you are out, especially with mixed drinks. You might be consuming more alcohol than you think.

Being aware of barriers to success

Withdrawal symptoms

Now you may already know them but please make yourself familiar with alcohol withdrawal symptoms. You don't need to be a heavy drinker to experience these. They can be mild, moderate, or severe and can lead to hallucinations and even death. Please really consider carefully if you need professional help. We suggest that you read Sylvain's chapter, Support Services & Alcohol Treatments, which explains the different kinds of expert support available. Some people end up drinking, even when they are doing well, just to stop the withdrawal symptoms. These symptoms do ease over time, but it is quite normal to expect grogginess and sleep disturbances as well as tummy troubles, headaches, irritability, and cravings. (8)

Boredom

You are going to find that you have got more time on your hands and boredom is often one of the reasons you might have been drinking. It is helpful if you think in advance about how you are going to spend that extra time. It's probably best not to embark on anything too drastic. Break time down into ten-minute activities perhaps. Could you paint nails or clean out that cupboard of doom? Maybe shop for something small. Apply a face-mask or clean the car, watch a TV show, or make that long-put-off phone call. Do anything. It doesn't have to cost a lot of money and it will help take your mind off the desire to have a drink or for the craving to pass.

Sugar cravings

There is a lot of sugar and calories in alcohol and sugar cravings can occur when you cut down. While it's not a great idea to eat too many unhealthy sweets in the long term and you really don't want to be replacing one bad habit with another, in the short-term, however, do what works for you. Do what is the least damaging to take the edge off as you cut down or withdraw from drinking. When Lesley was initially moderating her drinking, she would often find that if she had something to eat, the craving would pass. Instead of sweets, because of my diabetes, I chose frozen grapes, banana slices and berries.

Peer pressure

You may have decided and are feeling very committed to changing your drinking, however, social pressure from family and friends can make this difficult. It's likely you are going to be offered a drink at times when you really don't want one. This is an area where you need a bit of preparation. Have a polite, but convincing reply already rehearsed. The more quickly the offer is rejected, the less chance you'll give in to it. It's a bit like ripping the plaster off and hesitation allows you time to think of excuses to go along with the suggestion.

We tend to think of peer pressure as something that only affects young people, but how many times have you gone out and intended to order a non-alcoholic drink only to be told by your friends that one won't do you any harm, or that you are being boring? Have you ever confided in a friend that you are trying to cut down or abstain because you are worried about your intake, only to have them tell you that your drinking 'isn't really that bad'?

To cope with these pressures, you need to develop some resistance skills. This could be as simple as avoiding the event completely and not going to it. Realistically though you're probably not going to want to avoid socialising forever. Obviously, there will be times when you cannot or don't want to avoid those social activities, but again preplanning can help you get through them with your goals intact. (9, 10)

Consider if your beliefs are holding you back

There are many reasons why people believe they cannot stop or do not want to cut down. You've probably heard, or perhaps even used some of them yourself. Reasons such as:

- I can't imagine my life without alcohol
- I've had a hard day and I need to relax. I deserve a drink
- Life is no fun without drinking
- Everybody drinks
- I will be missing out if I don't drink
- I just don't have any willpower
- I'll have to avoid seeing my friends if I stop

I know when I was teaching, I used the 'I need to relax' and 'I've had a hard day and I deserve a drink' excuses a great deal. Which of these statements have you said to yourself and have you really given them the analysis they deserve? (11)

Relapses

Be kind to yourself. This will take time and you really don't need to be berating yourself if you do slip up. Doing that will not help you at all. Be kind.

Things you could do instead of drinking

Pamper yourself

Give yourself permission to have treats. If you've been drinking a lot, then you've probably been spending quite a bit of money on alcohol. Self-care is very important, and it isn't indulgent, it's very necessary.

Instead of spending the money on a drink, perhaps you could treat yourself to flowers, clothes or a movie, anything that makes you happy.

Discover healthy alternatives

If drinking has occupied a lot of your time in the past, then it is time to begin to fill your life with new healthy hobbies and activities. Reignite the passions you once had. What do you enjoy doing? If drinking has been your main pastime for years, go right back in time and ask yourself - what did you love doing when you were at school? What hobbies did you have? Try new things out.

Here are a few things to get you started that don't involve alcohol:

- Go for a walk or a run
- Spend time with a member of your family
- Start or join a book club
- Begin drawing or photography
- Try a new exercise
- Cook a healthy meal

The list really is infinite. (12)

Exercise

When I was in Sydney, during the first lockdown back in March 2020, and the gyms were closed, I started walking. I had no money, it was free and thankfully, still warm outside. I only did short distances at first but as the lockdown went on, I upped my mileage. I now try to set aside an hour and a half for a walk every day. With the pandemic and choosing not to go back into the classroom, I've made the decision to take those 90 minutes for myself, knowing that I am doing something for my health. This still leaves 1350 minutes remaining for me to get anything else that needs to be done in the day.

I can also honestly say that I believe walking has helped me. I choose not to drink as I want to get up early and feeling fresh for my morning walk. It has also helped me come to terms with Mum's death. While I'm out on my walk, I have the time to process my thoughts, about alcohol, about mum, and life in general and I have the 'me' time to work through my thoughts and feelings.

I've also started the BBC's Couch to 5K with Martin. It's something we can do together. To be honest, it is really, really tough and there are times when I just want to throw in the towel. Sarah Millican, a British comedienne, shouts in my ear and I try to run for the amount of time she suggests. We used to manage 10-kilometre runs in Singapore with its humidity and we were still drinking, so really, it can't be that hard, right?

Eat well

Another thing that I have been doing while I've been cutting down on the drink is cooking, and using an actual recipe which is something I've not been known to do. We have dined like royalty. There is nothing like whipping up a storm in the kitchen with the music turned up loudly. For the first time in years, my house is now also incredibly clean and tidy. I have got the time and organising my living space also acts as a distraction from grabbing a glass of something fizzy.

Rewards

Have a reward system in place and reward yourself at end of the week with a coffee - or something else such as a movie, a manicure or perhaps a round of golf? It might sound a bit like school-teacher speak, but this will be challenging and you deserve to reward yourself for a job well done.

Non-alcoholic alternatives

Alcohol-free drinks are getting better all the time. Find one that you enjoy. Just make sure that they aren't going to trigger you into wanting the real thing. Thanks to their arrival, it's a bit easier to blend in when you go out without making a big song and dance about what you are drinking. I've found most non-alcoholic wines were not to my taste and lacked the body you get from the real thing. There is, however, every reason to be hopeful that these will improve over time. You can expect to pay just as much for these when you go out, which is annoying, but I try to think of my drink as paying for the space - not just the beverage, to try and take the sting out of it. It's worthwhile exploring and asking for a low or no-alcohol alternative.

A goal of mine is to get in contact with some wine producers and ask them to try and produce a low or no-alcohol wine that tastes like wine, and not a child's blackcurrant drink. Websites such as www.zeroholic.co.uk or www.drydrinker.com have some great suggestions. Look at the options your local supermarket sells. They appear to be improving, both in quantity and quality, perhaps as demand for them increases. Again, it's all a matter of taste. Just as it is with alcohol. (13)

It's going to take planning

> *'If you always do what you've always done, you'll always get what you've always got.'*
>
> ~ Benjamin Franklin

Most people are more effective if they have some sort of plan. Some plans will be more detailed than others, and they will depend on what works best for you. Whatever you decide, please make sure you give your plan time for it to work. (14)

Other ideas to try

There are plenty of books, programs, and apps around to help you stop completely but that is not necessarily what we are advocating. Unless you decide that is absolutely what you want to do. It is worth pointing out that many people do in fact use moderation as a stepping-stone towards complete abstinence.

In summing up this chapter, I think the quote by Benjamin Franklin is a great one to finish on. It says what it needs to. Change something in your life to see change. Nothing will change if nothing is changed.

Try some of the suggestions but give them a good go. Like a well-known shampoo advertisement from home used to say, *'It won't happen overnight but it will happen'.* (15, 16)

A lifetime commitment may seem too daunting so take small, incremental steps and set a timeframe, say three months, to begin with. If you decide that something is not working, then try other alternatives. Just as you would with a gym class or a hairdresser that didn't suit. Keep trying different things. Something will eventually click and work for you and it may be a quick thing or it could take you some time. Hang in there.

Lesley Miller & Catheryn Kell-Clarke

Units and Measures of Alcohol

Cate

'Love like wine, gets better with time.'

~ unknown

By reconsidering your relationship with alcohol, you may have decided to consume less, or you may have chosen to stop completely. Whether you choose to cut down or stop completely, you are reducing the negative effects that alcohol can have on your body. Living in the UK, it made sense for me to look more deeply at what exactly the safe drinking recommendations are from the National Health Service or NHS.

Weekly recommendations

The UK Chief Medical Officer recommends that **both men and women drink no more than 14 units a week** on a regular basis. (1) I've often found that whenever I visited my GP, regardless of the reason, that question about how many units I was drinking always seemed to pop up. As a diabetic, I have regular consultations with my doctor, and when I lived in Singapore, I'd see my endocrinologist every three to four months. The question always came up, *'So Cate, how many units of alcohol are you drinking a week?'* Looking back, I am pretty sure I would have halved, if not quartered, the guesstimate I told my doctors. Perhaps you do the same?

What is a unit of alcohol?

We've all watched TV shows where the sad guy sits in the dingy bar and signals to a tired-looking barman for another shot. The barman then free pours him another glass of nondescript liquor. Or perhaps the scene is a group of women out on a Friday night drinking cocktails.

My point is, a shot is a shot is a shot. Right? That's what you may have thought but actually, no. Not all shots are the same, just as not all units of alcohol are equal either.

The other side to this sad bar scene is the classic Tom Cruise/Bryan Browne handsome barman combination. Spirits and mixers are thrown around skilfully to create something delicious in a frosted glass with a mini umbrella. Was anything measured? Is this real life? Did you know that when a cocktail is being made that all measures can go out the window? Not literally but **any** drink with more than three spirits is classed as a cocktail and any amount of alcohol may be added. This is up to each bar, and possibly even the bar person. This may explain why drinking two or three of this week's cocktail of choice in one establishment may have very little effect on you whereas at the bar next door, one drink alone could floor you.

Spirits

The UK government weights and measures law states:

'There are no specified quantities for sparkling wine or yellow wine by the glass or spirits other than gin, rum, vodka and whiskey' (2)

Put simply, any spirit other than gin, rum, vodka, and whiskey does not need to be measured. While I knew this from my pub days, seeing it again written in black and white, is quite scary. Essentially, you have no real idea about what measure or amount of alcohol you are drinking if your cocktail contains spirits other than the four mentioned. What spirits make up your favourite cocktail? Have you ever thought about how much alcohol goes into your drink?

Here's the maths

Here in the UK, one unit equals 10ml or 8g of pure alcohol. To determine how much alcohol is in a drink, based on its strength and size, the following equation is applied:

Strength (alcohol by volume or ABV) x **the volume of the drink** (in millilitres) ÷ **1,000** = the total number of units in your drink.

Using that calculation, the number of units in a pint (568mls) of 4% ABV beer, would be:

4 (ABV%) x 568 (ml) ÷ 1,000 = 2.3 units

A medium-sized glass, a 175ml of 13% ABV wine works out as:

13 (ABV%) x 175 (ml) ÷ 1,000 = 2.3 units

To calculate the number of units in a double gin and tonic, that's 50ml of gin with 40% ABV in a tall glass:

40 (ABV%) x 50 (ml) ÷ 1,000 = 2 units. (3)

As I mentioned in my chapter, I was knocking back gin and tonics with frightening regularity, probably around 10 or so units in one session if I'm being honest. I was so far over my weekly recommended limit, yet I wasn't viewed as some sad old soak. I was simply drinking, having a great time, and keeping up with the gang I was with. Oh boy!

As we've already mentioned, people often, either deliberately or unwittingly, misreport the number of units they may be consuming. A study conducted by researchers in 2013 at the University College in London, reported that when comparing alcohol sales figures with surveys of what people said they drank, there was a significant shortfall. In fact, slightly less than half of the alcohol sold was unaccounted for when compared to the consumption figures given by drinkers.

The researchers suggested that as many as 75 per cent of the people surveyed may have been drinking above the recommended daily alcohol limit. They reached these estimates by factoring in, the 'missing' alcohol, and found excess drinking was far more prevalent than was suggested by the official figures. The researchers proposed that much of the alcohol use went unreported, partly because drinkers did not want to admit to or keep track of how much they consumed.

(4) One can only imagine what statistics might show after the Covid-19 pandemic is over.

Alcohol by volume

Alcohol by Volume is abbreviated to ABV, abv, or alc/vol. It is a standard measure, used worldwide, of how much alcohol or ethanol is contained in an alcoholic beverage. This is expressed as a volume per cent and is defined as the number of millilitres (ml) of pure ethanol present in 100 ml. (5)

So, a typical ABV for gin ranges from 37.5 to 50 per cent meaning 37.5 to 50ml per 100ml is pure ethanol. Wines range from 5.5 to 16 per cent meaning 5.5 to 16ml of ethanol per 100ml. The average bottle of wine is 12.5 to 14.5 per cent. Beer varies greatly but generally begins at around three per cent.

Units of alcohol around the world.

Now not all units of alcohol are the same. There are variations around the world as to what exactly a unit is. As mentioned, here in the UK, one unit is defined as 10 ml or 8 grams of pure alcohol. (6) However, in the United States, a standard drink contains about 17.5ml or 14 grams of alcohol. (7) And just to confuse things even more, in New Zealand and Australia, one standard drink contains 12.5ml or 10 grams of pure alcohol. (8, 9)

Because different countries have different measures for one standard drink, this could explain why you've been on holiday somewhere exotic and your tipple of choice may have left you with a raging hangover the next morning. Thinking, pre-Covid-19, about your favourite holiday destination, did you know how much alcohol you were consuming? Maybe something to consider on your next holiday when you ask for your usual drink.

Added confusion

The countries I've lived in, all had their own little alcohol quirks. New Zealand with its enormous shed-like pubs, represents to me the comfort of the familiar with the world-famous Sauvignon Blancs and the beers from my childhood. Australia has crazy names and glass sizes; a pony, which is about half a pint, or 140ml, a schooner which is about three-quarters of a pint or 425ml and a middy which is almost half a pint, or 285 ml. There are all these different measurements and each state often calls it something completely different. A Kiwi in a bar asking for a beer in a glass was always going to be given a hard time. Believe me. I'd rather keep it simple, although it could be handy information for when you're travelling down under on your next holiday.

Drinking in Singapore was a real eye-opener; the cost of alcohol was mind-boggling. Twenty Singapore dollars, or around £10 for a glass of pretty average, often chilled, red wine. Offset this with the high salaries and a low tax rate, the price was, however, no deterrent to me and my teacher friends. Because we had a high, disposable income. We were, looking back now, spending up large and drinking with frightening regularity.

It can be mind-boggling, can't it? I was confused about units and measurements and I had worked in the hospitality industry. Why was there so much difference? I'd only just scratched the surface. A general rule of thumb that most people go by is that **it takes about one hour for the body to break down or metabolise one British unit of alcohol.** As I've already mentioned, one standard drink in the United States is 17.5ml or 14 grams, approximately 1.75 units of alcohol, meaning this will take your body about an hour and three-quarters to process. One drink! Yikes!

How are units and drinking alcohol connected?

Let's look at what a unit looks like and what it can do to your body. As mentioned, many of us don't really know how much we're drinking as we are confused about alcoholic measurements.

1- 2 units:

- A small 125 ml glass of 12% wine contains 1.5 units
- A bottle (330ml) of 5% strength lager/beer/cider contains 1.7 units

Impact: After drinking one to two units of alcohol, you feel relaxed, your heart rate will speed up and your blood vessels will expand. You may become warm, sociable and talkative, the feelings that are associated with moderate drinking.

4 - 6 units:

- 2 x 175 ml glasses of 12% wine are about 4.2 units
- 2 pints of 5.2% strength lager/beer/cider is 6 units

Impact: Your brain and nervous system will begin to be affected. Your judgement and decision-making could become compromised and you may become more reckless and uninhibited. You could become lightheaded as the alcohol impairs the cells in your nervous system and your reaction times and coordination are adversely affected. You will start dehydrating which is one of the causes of a hangover. Upon reflection, this is quite a reaction to not really a large amount of drinking.

8 - 9 units:

- 6 x 125ml glasses of 12% wine are 9 units

- 3 x 250ml glasses of 12% wine are 9 units
- Around three pints of beer is around 9 units
- 5 bottles (330ml) of 5% strength lager/beer/cider are 8.5 units

Impact: Your reaction times will start to slow, and your speech may become slurred. You may experience changes in your time perception and you could be moving more slowly. Your vision becomes less focused and your liver is unable to remove all the alcohol. You may be more emotional and you'll most probably wake up with a hangover.

10 - 12 units:

- 4 x 250 ml glasses of 12% wine are 12 units
- 6 bottles (330ml) of 5% strength lager/beer/cider are 10.2 units

Impact: Your co-ordination can be very diminished, and you could be at risk of having a serious accident. You may be drowsy due to the high level of alcohol having a depressant effect on both your mind and body. This level of alcohol, over time, can begin to reach lethal levels. Your body will attempt to get rid of the alcohol by passing it out in your urine. Unless the fluids are replaced, this all contributes to you feeling very dehydrated the following morning, often with a severe headache. Your digestion may be upset with either diarrhoea or constipation. You may also experience nausea, vomiting, and indigestion.

12+ units:

- 5 x 250ml glasses of 12% wine or just over one and a half bottles of wine are 15 units
- 5 pints of 5.2% strength lager/beer/cider is 15 units

Impact: When you drink more than 12 units, you may be putting yourself at a considerable risk of alcohol poisoning, especially if you drink quickly. Automatic functions of your body such as breathing, your heart rate and the gag reflex, which prevents you from choking, are seriously impaired by the alcohol. At this level of drinking, you could fall into a coma, which may lead to death. (10, 11)

So, as you can see, it's really not that difficult to drink more than the recommended **14 units per week**. Please keep in mind that some people such as women, younger drinkers and those with small builds may experience the effects listed after consuming smaller amounts of alcohol.

The NHS recommends that:

- Men and women are advised not to drink more than **14 units** a week on a regular basis

- Spread your drinking over 3 or more days if you regularly drink as much as 14 units a week

- If you want to cut down, try to have several drink-free days each week (12)

The chapter, Alcohol and Your Body, looks in greater detail at what alcohol does to the specific parts of your body. There is a great deal of information around about calculating units of alcohol and I strongly recommend you conduct some research into your drink of choice. I have to admit, investigating this chapter was eye-opening and very scary. It helped to convince me that I had indeed made the right decision by cutting down on my alcohol intake.

Lesley Miller & Catheryn Kell-Clarke

Sylvain

'The gem cannot be polished without friction, nor the person perfected without trials.'

~ Chinese proverb

Let me take you on a unique journey which started in the early seventies in a tiny village in the western region of the Ivory Coast in West Africa. Looking back, I realise that like Cate, I too discovered alcohol early, sometime before my tenth birthday. I was the fourth child in a family of eight children and the first boy. This gave me the special privilege of being 'Daddy's Boy', and I was made to feel special as my parents had longed for a son after three daughters.

As such, I became a constant companion to my late father, who was a very hard-working farmer. I was exposed to his passions which were working in the field, helping people, providing for his family, and hunting. He would work in the fields from sunrise to sunset. My whole world was my tiny red soiled, dusty village called Teisson. I would often walk barefoot or half-naked, wearing only shorts, not because of the lack of clothing, but because the sun was perpendicular to the Earth and you could record temperatures of 38-40°C in the shade.

Growing up in Teisson was fun, but it meant that my father-son relationship was rather different to anything you would experience in the Western world, hence my early introduction to alcohol. My dad loved to drink, rather a lot, as it turned out, and this meant that I drank too.

I discovered alcohol when I was only nine. Like all little boys in my community, I drank the local palm wine, which was a sweet, high-quality drink produced by my father. Fresh palm wine is a drink that is believed to have nutritious properties and it would be given to children to drink. When palm wine is not fermented, it is non-alcoholic, and I used to enjoy drinking it for its sweetness. However, as I grew up, I started to drink a stronger palm wine and I realised that it was making me tipsy. I liked that new feeling. The sweet taste quickly became boring, and it was referred to as being 'girly'. I was now drinking for the buzz, although I did not realise this at the time. I liked the way it made me feel.

The truth is that I did not like the hard work that we were doing on the farm and I was taking cover behind drinking palm wine, which was making me sleep while my siblings were working under the sun. I think my laziness on the farm made me study hard at school to avoid working hard in the field like my parents and other siblings.

Palm wine is a very popular drink in West Africa and is usually used for recreational consumption. It is also used for ceremonies such as weddings and funerals. The palm wine is the juice that is obtained by scarring the inner part of the palm tree and is collected in a container such as a clay pot, plastic, or glass jar. The juice is sweet at first because of the sugar, but this turns into alcohol with time, as the sugar ferments. There are stories of children who had lost their mothers at birth and were fed on freshly tapped palm wine. They survived - proof of its nutritious substance.

As a teenager, I left my local community and moved to the city to attend secondary school, college, and later university. At this stage, I was going out at the weekend with my friends and drinking beer or wine. Back in the village, we used to get drunk and do funny things such as hanging dead snakes on trees to scare girls or hide in bushes to startle our friends. We were just being silly boys, but we were not causing serious trouble.

My drinking in the city was sporadic and not much to worry about, as at most, I would have three glasses of wine or four beers on a night out. I still remember going home drunk and waking up with a hangover on one or two occasions. My drinking increased gradually, and with it, my tolerance, but I never drank on weekdays as I needed to go to college and do my homework.

After four years at secondary school and three years in college, I started university in the capital city Abidjan, and I lived on the campus. I was older and I had a new set of friends who I drank with, not only at weekends and on special occasions but also on weekdays. We were drinking in the local bars and restaurants around the campus but having drinks in our rooms was out of the question. I used to drink with my friends for fun and I never experienced any problem with alcohol.

In the city, I also discovered other drinks, such as low strength beers and lagers, wines and spirits. At college and university, I would go partying and clubbing with my friends. Because birthday parties and exam result celebrations were commonplace amongst the students, my alcohol consumption increased, and before long, I was drinking almost everything I could get my hands on. Nevertheless, money was scarce in those days, so alcohol was not always available.

When I started working as a police officer in the mid-nineties, I was able to afford to drink more. I would have a couple of drinks with my colleagues after work, and then I'd have a couple more when I got home, either relaxing in front of the television or with dinner. I guess my drinking could have been described as moderate or social drinking because I could do without alcohol for days or weeks without experiencing any withdrawal symptoms. I was not drinking every day either, but I was having more than the recommended 'safest' limit of 14 units per week.

Alcohol consumption in West Africa can be blamed for some road traffic accidents. There are also cases of addicts who fail to financially maintain their families because of drink, and it has also been linked to crime and domestic violence, just as in other countries. But the scale of the alcohol problem was small where I lived, and alcohol addiction was not a public health concern as far as I am aware. Probably the only thing stopping me from becoming an alcoholic was the fact that I was holding down a responsible job.

In December 1999, my world was turned upside down by the military coup in the Ivory Coast, and I was forced to leave both my job and my country behind. Life, in general, took a rapid turn for the worse. The military took over the civilian government and took matters into their own hands. Justice and human rights were put in jeopardy. There were a lot of extra judiciary killings, and impunity became the norm. I felt that it was not safe enough to carry on working as a police officer or to even live peacefully in these conditions, but I continued working before I left the country.

I moved to the UK in December 2000. It snowed for two days solid after my arrival and I convinced myself that I needed shots of brandy every morning and evening simply to maintain my body temperature. Looking back, I was probably drinking so much because I was traumatised. My new home felt lonely, even though I had my sister and her boyfriend in the UK. It certainly didn't help that I couldn't speak English.

One thing that I still remember is that I noticed a much wider selection of alcoholic drinks than I'd ever seen in Africa. I was also struck by the fact that I couldn't find any of the drinks that I used to enjoy at home, not even the fancy ones that we'd had in the city of Abidjan. Once I was settled, my drinking really reduced, partly because I couldn't find any of my usual favourites, but also because I was staying with a Muslim family who didn't approve of alcohol. I started to drink more once I had my own place. I remember drinking a 70cl bottle of Jack Daniels by myself on one occasion and around this time, I also started to drink cider, beer, wine, whiskey, gin, rum, and brandy.

Before I dive into how I became a practitioner, I think it is useful to share what I now believe made me opt for my chosen career. Years ago, I would not have been able to answer this question but through time and experience, I have come to admit that my late father had an alcohol problem. This is to say that he was drinking palm wine on a regular basis and I would rate its alcohol content at being anything between five and 12 per cent. My father's drinking was a habit, or a necessity, as he used to describe it. He was not drinking with friends to have fun or to socialise.

There would be periods when my dad was quiet for weeks without any arguments and fights. There were also numerous times when he would argue with my maternal grandmother and mother over his drinking. He used to drink early in the morning, the time when palm wine tappers usually go to collect their first batches. Palm wine is collected three times a day; morning, afternoon, and evening and my father would drink about a litre of palm wine on each of these occasions every day.

My father worked in the fields and I never saw him break once for breakfast or lunch. He usually had only one meal a day, and that was in the evening when he came home. He used to work in the fields from Monday to Saturday. Sunday was his day off from work, but not from palm wine.

As a young boy, I witnessed scenes of domestic violence where my mum was assaulted by my dad as they had regular arguments. There were scenes that could now be interpreted as alcohol-induced psychosis or episodes of schizophrenia. I can still remember how my dad once kicked a pot of stew that was being cooked, and my mum had to salvage some pieces of meat and the other ingredients from the floor to feed us.

The arguments with my granny and my mum were frequent. My siblings and I were ashamed of my dad's drinking because he would shout so much that everyone in the village knew what was happening. After a few drinks, he would sit in our compound and complain loudly about different things, such as politics and injustice.

One day, my paternal uncle came from the city to take my dad to a rehab centre for six months. I later learnt that he was taken to a psychiatric hospital, probably because of alcohol-induced mental health issues, or maybe the issues that led to the onset of his drinking in the first place.

On his return to the village, he was meant to remain abstinent, and everyone celebrated his recovery. By then, when I was about 12 or 13, I remember being happy about having a fresh start. However, my dad started to drink again, and everyone was disappointed. He continued to drink until the civil war broke out in the Ivory Coast in 2002. As the rebels entered my region and our village, my family fled, and my dad found himself in Abidjan where he was not able to produce his own palm wine.

I cannot say exactly why he stopped drinking, but I know that he stopped five or six years before he passed away at 69 in 2006. By then, my grandma had died, and we children were adults. My mum was happy to see her husband recover and not to have to put up with any more of the arguments and fights. I guess her last memories of him are positive ones. Despite his alcohol problems we loved our dad dearly and he loved us too.

I am guessing it was his experience that informed my career path. In 2005, I was visiting my sister in Sheffield when I came across an article in the local newspaper which advertised a CBT drug and alcohol counselling course. Apparently, there was a shortage of alcohol and drug counsellors, and I felt like this was my calling. So, I resigned from my full-time job as a postman in London and moved to Sheffield to study drug and alcohol counselling at Sheffield Hallam University.

This course was a part-time Level 4 Higher Education Certificate in drug and alcohol counselling. By then, I'd only been in the UK for five years, and I was still struggling a little with English. I was the only black person on the course, but luckily, my fellow students and the tutors were incredibly helpful, and I was determined to complete my studies.

After two years, I graduated, and I started working in the drug and alcohol field. I took a job in 2007 as a Band 4 drug and alcohol worker within the NHS. I worked as a recovery practitioner, receiving referrals, and assessing adults with alcohol and drug problems. I was supporting them through interventions such as motivational interviewing, one to one counselling and relapse prevention. I was also helping people with budgeting skills and signposting them to other agencies such as GP surgeries, job centres, and housing offices. It was surprising to see how chaotic peoples' lives can become when they are addicted to drugs or alcohol.

It was tough at times, and I did experience some racism. I was often asked 'what I was doing' in the UK which I did find difficult, but I persevered. In total, I worked for seven drug and alcohol service providers in both Sheffield and London for over 16 years, which has enabled me to acquire a great deal of knowledge and experience. I have attended countless in-house and external training sessions which have all helped to shape my understanding of alcohol.

I can honestly say that, in my opinion, the alcohol problem in the UK is far worse than it is in the Ivory Coast. British people can afford to buy alcohol, and it is widely available, cheap and comes in high strengths. In contrast, fewer people can afford to buy alcohol in the Ivory Coast. Many people drink low strength local beers and wines. However, some people do also produce and drink rum which can be more than 60 per cent in strength.

I would also say from my observations that I think there are more issues with isolation, loneliness, boredom, and mental disorders in the UK than there are in the Ivory Coast, which we know are contributory factors in people drinking too much. The majority of people in West

Africa, as far as I know, drink for fun, or to socialise rather than use alcohol as a coping mechanism.

Drinking in West Africa was seen as a 'man thing'. When I was growing up, women who drank used to keep a low profile. However, this has now changed, and women are drinking more and more and even competing with the men, just as Lesley and her friends were doing back in the UK in the 'nineties. The younger generations appear to be much more swayed by the alcohol industry's marketing and promotions. The drinking culture in the Ivory Coast is shifting dangerously, as more young people, including students and pupils, are drinking during school hours and weekends. There is also a trend of buying cheap alcohol in small plastic bags which is easily accessible and easy to carry.

There is still definitely a stigma attached to alcoholism in West Africa just as there is in most countries. Someone with a drinking problem will be marginalised and mocked. There are often incidents of drinkers being victims of unprovoked verbal and physical aggression. The alcohol industry is targeting more the younger generations and women with new products, as already discussed in the previous chapters. This policy has paid off as these populations are drinking not only openly and freely but they are increasing in numbers. This may suggest that in the next decades we could see a further increase in the number of women and young people drinking alcohol.

As a child, drinking the sweet palm wine was fun for me. I really liked the taste. However, when I became a teenager, I drank alcohol because it was making me feel tipsy and I enjoyed socialising with my friends. I never discovered the relaxing side of alcohol as I always associated alcohol with fun.

Now I do drink a shot or two of whiskey or brandy, or perhaps one or two glasses of wine sometimes to unwind from a long day of work. My drinking has not really changed in the last 20 years, and I do try to keep a careful watch over how many units I am getting through. During the 2020 lockdown, I started to order wine online, which I shared with my family at lunch, dinner, and on special occasions. I also buy spirits and beers from supermarkets and I do keep alcohol in my house. Nevertheless, I choose and decide what to drink, when to drink and how much I drink, perhaps because I know how easily alcohol problems can take hold and how destructive they can be.

Alcohol Reconsidered

Alcohol and Your Body

Cate & Sylvain

'Drink sir, is a great provoker of three things... nose painting, sleep and urine. Lechery, sir, it provokes, and unprovokes; it provokes the desire but takes away the performance.'

~ William Shakespeare

Now that you have some understanding about ABVs and units of alcohol, this seems the right place to look at what alcohol can do to your body. It's not particularly comfortable reading so take it slowly and in small pieces because it is important.

Again, Lesley and I can't reiterate this enough, please check with your doctor or health advisor if you have any medical concerns about your relationship with alcohol.

The taste of alcohol

Your first taste of alcohol may have been nasty. Do you remember it? What was it? How did it make you feel?

As I have already mentioned, my first taste of alcohol would have been a few sips of dad's evening beer. I liked the fizz and the colour of the beer-but I wasn't, from memory, that keen on the taste which would have been very bitter to my young palate.

In a bid to lure young drinkers, many drink manufacturers add sweeteners to their products. (1) Although the research is inconsistent, the NHS suggests that using artificial sweeteners may stimulate the appetite and can play a role in weight gain. (2) So, does drinking artificially sweetened alcoholic drinks at a young age help to contribute to the world's growing obesity epidemic? Food for thought. Think about the sweet alco-pops on our supermarket shelves. Who are they aimed at with their bright colours and catchy names? Probably not at you, with your now more sophisticated palate. No, they're aimed at the younger drinkers who haven't yet experienced the highs and lows of drinking. Think back to when you were younger. What were you drinking? How does that compare to now? Once hooked on the taste of alcohol, the marketing companies can hit impressionable youngsters with other alcoholic treats.

It comes down to getting that first taste because, after the first couple of mouthfuls, the feelings associated with alcohol begin to kick in; the sensation of warmth, the confidence to talk to strangers more easily and that feeling of being relaxed. If you gave a young or new drinker a glass of your favourite bubbles or a malty real ale, they'd most probably dislike it and possibly even spit it out. They haven't developed the taste for it yet. However, once they begin to realise the effects that this liquid can have on their body, they are more than likely to begin to develop a taste for it. (3)

Alcohol and your body systems

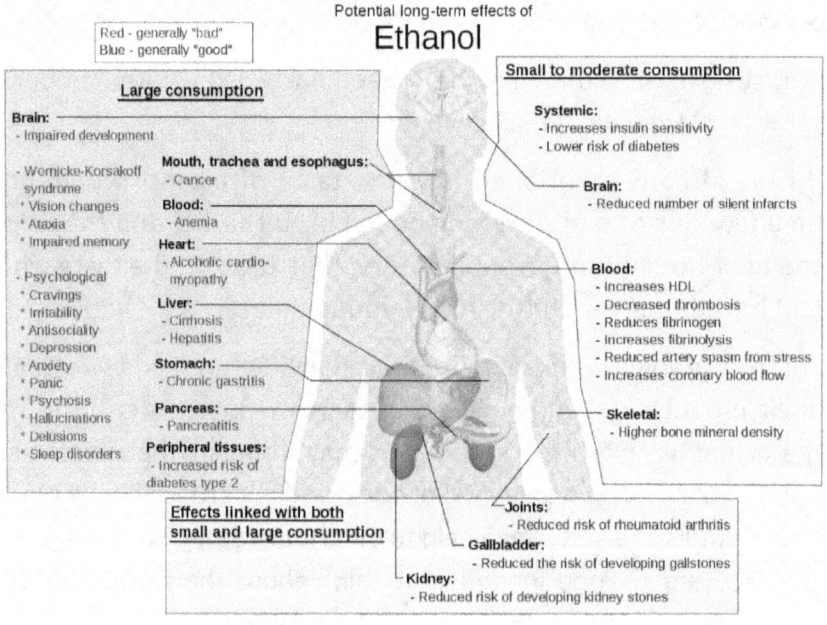

By Mikael Häggström, used with permission

Drinking more than the recommended amounts can cause many issues and can increase the risks of some cancers. These include; mouth, gullet, liver, colon, and breast, as well as sexual difficulties such as impotence. Alcohol can also exacerbate mental health conditions such as depression, anxiety, sleep issues, panic attacks and chronic fatigue. It may also delay recovery.

Regularly drinking too much alcohol dramatically increases your risks of long-term damage to your health. It quadruples the risks of diseases like hypertension or high blood pressure in men and doubles the risk for women. The risk in the case of a stroke sees a doubling for men and an increase by four times in women. Another nasty, coronary heart disease sees 1.7 times increased risk for males and 1.3 times for females. Pancreatitis, which is an inflammation of the pancreas, is tripled in men and doubled for women. For both men and women, heavy drinking increases your risk of liver disease by 13 times. A very unlucky number indeed. (4)

Your nervous system

Alcohol molecules are very small and as such, can enter your blood system very quickly. Alcohol affects several parts of your brain; it contracts brain tissues and can destroy brain cells. It depresses your central nervous system. Long-term drinking can also cause serious problems with your cognition and memory. (5)

Your circulatory system

The link between regular drinking and having high blood pressure is clear. High blood pressure puts a strain on your heart, which, is at the end of the day, just a muscle, albeit a very important one. High blood pressure, can lead to cardiovascular disease. This in turn can increase your risk of a heart attack and stroke.

Alcohol, particularly red wine, has been said to be beneficial for the heart and it has been linked with a lower risk of coronary heart disease. However, the risks usually outweigh any possible benefits, although the advice changes with quite alarming regularity. Recent research from the British Heart Foundation revealed that the only real benefits are for women who are over the age of 55 and drink around five units of alcohol a week. This is approximately 2 and a half 175 ml glasses of wine or 3 x 330 ml bottles of beer a week.

A word of caution

When it comes to research, not all studies are equal. You may find some of the drink companies commission the statistics, so you need to be cautious about what you read and who you choose to believe.

Remember there is no medical reason to start drinking alcohol if you don't already, and there is no drink, such as red wine or beer, that can be proven to be deemed 'better' for your health. (6,7)

Your digestive system

Researching for this chapter meant a great deal of reading, during which I came across a piece by the Association of Registered Colon Hydrotherapists called, *'Booze and Poos! What alcohol does to your digestive system!'* What an intriguing title. I had to find out more. As mentioned before, alcohol will do one of two things, it will either speed things up or slow things down.

Alcohol increases the speed that your stomach empties into your small intestine. The digestive waste then moves along quickly to your large intestine, too quickly for all the water to be absorbed. Couple this with extra unabsorbed water alongside the additional fluid you're consuming, and things are going to get mushy. An unpleasant side-effect resulting in an urgent need to rush to the toilet. Diarrhoea is common, but if this persists for more than two days, you really should seek medical help.

Did you know that if your stomach empties too quickly, it can release undigested carbohydrates into your small intestines which then feed undesirable microbes? This could cause an imbalance in your sensitive gut flora and again, the possibility of stomach upsets. The occasional tipple won't cause this, but it can be a problem for more regular drinkers.

The opposite of speeding things up in the gut department, slowing things right down. To a stop. Constipation. Alcohol is a diuretic so although you may be producing more urine during a drinking session, you are taking in less fluid and so can become dehydrated. This excess urination can also lead to you losing essential electrolytes such as sodium and potassium. These electrolytes are needed to help you retain fluid in your body and your stools. This can all lead to the 'dry-horrors' when you wake up the next morning with a dry mouth and an enormous thirst. Alcohol can also be a common trigger for flare-ups in digestive system diseases, such as Crohn's Disease and Irritable Bowel Syndrome, (8, 9)

Alcohol is not great for your waistline as mentioned. Losing weight this year has been much easier, and I say this from experience, without as many added alcohol calories.

The calorie equivalents in alcohol are quite terrifying. The following information and much more can be found in the NHS resource, 'How Much Is Too Much?'

- 175 ml of white wine = 130 calories or a bag of crisps
- 175 ml of red wine = 120 calories or a slice of cheese and tomato pizza
- A pint of lager or beer = 170 calories or a small sausage roll

- A pint of cider = 200 calories or a mince pie
- A shot of tequila = 160 calories or a doughnut
- A 275ml bottle of alcopop = 200 calories or a chicken drumstick

(10)

I'd hate to add up the number of calories I've drunk. Enough totalling a banquet fit for the Queen no doubt!

Your reproductive system

Alcohol isn't as sexy as is often thought. In fact, it often leads to a good number of problems in the bedroom. In men, it can affect the all-important testosterone levels. Too much alcohol may also lead to lowered sperm count and impotence. Alcohol can disrupt the menstrual cycle in women and may even stop a woman from conceiving. (11)

Pretty terrifying reading. Hands up who hasn't had a night out on the lash and either lost count of the amount you were drinking or didn't really care?

A drink can be damaging enough on its own, but its effects can be very dangerous when mixed with other substances.

Alcohol and nicotine

In smoking two things can happen. Firstly, you inhale smoke which sends carbon dioxide to your lungs, resulting in a sensation of dizziness which can intensify the feelings of being drunk. Secondly, as you absorb nicotine, which is a stimulant drug that balances the depressive effects of alcohol, you need to drink more to feel drunk. This is why people tend to drink more when they are burning through the cigarettes. Tobacco and alcohol work together to damage the cells of the body, multiplying the damage. The cancer-causing chemicals in tobacco are more easily absorbed by the mouth and the throat when combined with alcohol.

Alcohol and marijuana (cannabis)

Cannabis and alcohol when used together can have unpredictable physical and psychological results. Having alcohol in your bloodstream can potentially cause your body to absorb the active ingredient tetrahydrocannabinol (THC) faster which can lead to cannabis having a much stronger effect. Physically, you can experience dizziness, nausea, and vomiting, while the psychological effects can include panic, anxiety, or paranoia. 'Skunk', is a slang term for stronger types of cannabis, and it can pose even greater risks, because it may contain three times as much THC. Cannabis is usually smoked with tobacco which, of course, can increase your risk of cancer. (12)

Alcohol and cocaine

A common but particularly dangerous partnership is alcohol and cocaine. Together they increase the risk of heart attacks, fits and even sudden death. An extremely poisonous substance called cocaethylene is produced in your liver when these two drugs interact. This can increase the depressive effects of alcohol, making your reaction to cocaine stronger. You are also more likely to be aggressive with this substance in your body. Your heart and liver are exposed to a longer period of stress because cocaethylene takes longer to get out of your system than alcohol or cocaine. Mixing alcohol and cocaine can kill you up to 12 hours after you've absorbed the mix.

In most users, cocaethylene produces euphoria and its effects are longer-lasting than cocaine alone. Some studies suggest that consuming alcohol with cocaine may be more cardiotoxic, which means there is an 18-25% more risk of a heart attack from cocaethylene than cocaine alone. Cocaethylene has a higher affinity for the dopamine transporter meaning it creates more euphoria than cocaine. (13)

Alcohol and ecstasy (MDMA)

Alcohol may reduce the 'high' felt from ecstasy while it is in your system, but the next day, when you 'come down', you will feel much worse if you have been drinking. Together they can be deadly and a severe hangover is one of the milder side-effects when combining these two drugs. Ecstasy dehydrates you as does alcohol and the risk of overheating and becoming seriously dehydrated is likely.

Most ecstasy-related deaths involve alcohol, and many deaths result from heatstroke as fluids lost through long dance periods in hot clubs have not been replaced. As alcohol is a diuretic, which means it makes you go to the bathroom a lot and sweat more, it's even harder to keep enough fluid in your body when you drink it while using ecstasy. There is also a greater strain put on your liver and kidneys when you combine the two drugs. As with many other combinations, you're likely to experience nausea and vomiting. (14)

Alcohol and amphetamines

Using amphetamines, or 'speed' has been likened to an adrenalin rush where your breathing, blood pressure and heart rate all speed up. As with ecstasy, amphetamines may also cause your body temperature to increase which can lead to dehydration when alcohol is included in the mix.

As amphetamines already put pressure on your heart, by adding alcohol, this pressure can be fatal. Emotions may be intensified and inhibitions lost by combining these two drugs, and you may end up behaving in a way you could seriously regret. Under the influence of amphetamines, you may feel more confident or energised, but you can easily become anxious, paranoid, or aggressive, particularly when you add alcohol to the mix. You don't feel the full effects of alcohol until the amphetamines have worn off. Mixing the two means you can drink dangerous amounts of alcohol without realising. (15)

Alcohol and heroin

One of the most dangerous combinations of drugs is that of alcohol and heroin. Heroin is a 'downer'. They are depressants. That is to say, they depress the central nervous system and slow down vital functions such as heart rate and breathing. Heroin when combined with alcohol, which is also a downer, is essentially doubling up and putting yourself at risk of overdosing. The National Treatment Agency for Substance Misuse, here in the UK, proposes that even small amounts of alcohol can lower the amount of heroin needed to fatally overdose. Around three-quarters of people who die from heroin overdoses have also been drinking alcohol as well. (16)

Alcohol and 'legal highs'

Previously known as 'legal highs', drugs such as mephedrone or 'meow meow' actually became illegal in 2010 when they were classified as class B drugs. It is a powerful stimulant and this group of drugs is closely related to amphetamines. They are derived from the plant khat, commonly used as a stimulant in East Africa and have similar effects to ecstasy and amphetamines. These drugs may make you anxious and paranoid and can overstimulate your circulation, damage the heart, speed up the nervous system and may cause fits. As with any drug that produces a 'high', combine them with alcohol and you are at risk of everything from nausea and vomiting to coma and death. (17)

Lesley Miller & Catheryn Kell-Clarke

Alcohol and Your Mind

Lesley

'If you know someone who tries to drown their sorrows, you might tell them sorrows know how to swim.'

~ H. Jackson Brown Jr.

Before we go any further, it would probably be a good idea to really think about what we are talking about when we are referring to mental health. The term 'wellbeing' seems to have become part of our vocabulary over recent years. It is possible that you may have seen more focus on this in your workplace and if not at work, then you will certainly have been the target of some marketing on social media. Let's not forget 'wellbeing' isn't just a way of health experts trying to place equal importance on mental and physical health. It is also an industry thought to be globally worth $4.2 trillion a year. (1)

It's easy for us to compartmentalise physical and mental health and see them as two separate issues, as we have done historically, when of course, they are interlinked. For example, when was the last time you fancied going to the gym when you had a hangover? Exactly. But what is 'mental health', and what has alcohol got to do with it?

What is mental health?

The World Health Organisation defines mental health as:

'...a state of well-being in which every individual realizes his or her potential, can cope with the normal stresses of life, can work productively and fruitfully, and is able to make a contribution to his/her community.' (2)

It goes on to explain that mental health is determined by a range of socio-economic, biological and environmental factors and states that

there is no health without mental health. It will not come as a surprise to anyone that an unhealthy lifestyle is associated with poor mental health and let's be honest, no amount of exercise or healthy eating cancels out drinking too much.

Alcohol and emotional wellbeing

I am guessing that if I asked you whether heavy alcohol consumption can negatively affect mental health, you wouldn't hesitate in agreeing that it could. You are probably all too aware, from personal experience, of how alcohol can be detrimental to mental health. Whether you have suffered a catalogue of minor indignations from your drinking, or have committed some alcohol-induced atrocity and reached rock bottom, you know what it feels like to be drinking more than you are happy with. It is likely to be impacting at least one aspect of your wellbeing, whether the effect is emotional, social, intellectual, physical, or even occupational.

An important question to ask yourself is to what extent is your drinking affecting your mental health and is it a price worth paying? If the answer is 'no', then why would you continue? It's a question I used to ask myself a lot.

Why do we drink?

It is important to reflect on why we are drinking because if we can begin to pinpoint the reasons, we are more likely to do something about it. At present in the UK, it is thought that there are an estimated 586,780 dependent drinkers, which sounds like a woeful underestimate to me. Only 18 per cent of these people are receiving treatment. (3) Why is that? Are the other 82 per cent in denial or are they simply unaware of treatments and interventions that are available?

All kinds of factors can influence our drinking. Social drinkers consume alcohol to celebrate, to be convivial and to be, well, sociable. Those drinking to cope are doing so to escape and to avoid and regulate unpleasant emotions. I would argue that, upon reflection, I was doing both.

Researchers found that those drinking alcohol to 'cope' are more likely to find themselves problem drinking, but both groups are at risk. (4) I'm sure if you look back at your own drinking, you would agree that this makes sense.

What are your triggers?

If you are anything like me, it will be the drinking that you are doing to 'cope' that you will be wanting to change. It is worth thinking about which drinks are causing you the most problems. Does the type of drinking you are doing change at different times during the week? Going out for a few drinks after work was far less problematic for me than the solo drinking to excess every evening.

Our reasons for drinking are complex and might not always be the same. We don't always fit neatly into boxes. In reality, your relationship with alcohol is likely to change at various points in your life, depending on what is happening and who your friends are at the time. How much those close to you drink may influence you too.

What does moderation mean to you?

Cate and I have discussed this. She likened it to being on a strict diet where one little slip can equal disaster. This is why we need to explore what moderation can mean in a positive light and what it means on a longer-term basis, rather than just looking at the days and week ahead. What does moderation mean to you in the longer term? It might mean having two days off drinking a week, or it could mean reducing how much you drink each day. Maybe you are thinking about cutting units on a weekly basis or perhaps opting for lower alcohol alternatives. I found setting myself realistic targets helpful as it stopped me throwing the baby out with the bath water if I did slip up.

Keep trying

Relapse, or slipping up is a very normal part of changing your drinking but this is still portrayed by the media as a failure. 'Falling off the wagon', is the expression commonly used to describe someone who was having a relapse, which I think we can all agree, is not particularly helpful.

It was the social benefits which made it so difficult to reduce my drinking, and they are why I am sure that I don't want to abstain altogether. Most societies throughout time have had the equivalent of a pub and alcohol is indelibly linked to fun, and that can be hard to turn your back on. Of course, if one drink is going to send you off on a massive bender, then it might be better to give up completely.

Why the pub can be good for us

It will come as no surprise to hear that I have always loved a pub. This is even more true at the time of writing as our pubs have been closed for most of the last 12 months due to the Covid-19 pandemic. I used to joke that I could remain abstinent forever, provided I never went out again. It doesn't take much of a leap of the imagination to see how drinking can affect your mental health in a negative way, but does it provide any benefits?

In 2017, researchers at the University of Oxford looked at whether having a drink improved social cohesion. Professor Robin Dunbar from Oxford's Experimental Psychology Department said:

'This study showed that frequenting a local pub can directly affect people's social network size and how engaged they are with their local community, which in turn can affect how satisfied they feel in life.' (5)

It is probably true that if you look hard enough for the research you can prove anything, but this does ring true. It is worth pointing out though that this research was funded by the Campaign for Real Ale, CAMRA. (6) As Cate said, it's always worth looking at who is funding the research and why the findings might be to their advantage.

Find your motivation

Sylvain talks later about the 'Cycle of Change', and when he first told me about it, it really resonated. Like everybody else, I couldn't change my drinking because I thought other people wanted me to. I had to do it because I wanted to.

My main motivating factor was fear. I was scared that I was slowly killing myself and I was sick of feeling emotionally numb. In all honesty, I hadn't really spent much time thinking about how alcohol consumption affected my mental health, because I had just accepted that being a teacher and a single parent was just always going to be stressful.

One study looked at what experiences would motivate people to reduce the amount they drink. As you might imagine, younger participants gave reasons from physical health, injuries, sexual regret, and trouble with the police. Older participants were more likely to cite reasons such as social embarrassment, forgetfulness, physical health and family reasons. (7)

Chicken or egg?

If you are drinking too much, too often, there is a good chance that you might suffer from anxiety and/or depression, and that drinking might be your way of 'self-medicating'. The decades seem to fly by, and it's unusual for anyone to get through life without experiencing some of life's traumas. It's easy to get used to having a few drinks to take the edge off. For others, the reverse is true. Their drinking actually leads to poor mental health. This leads to the ultimate chicken or egg question.

If you are drinking a lot and you are feeling anxious or depressed, you need to ask yourself which came first – the booze or the poor mental health? Depression and drinking have a mutually reinforcing relationship, meaning that if you experience one, you have got more chance of experiencing the other. (8)

Depression

Depression is another alarmingly common problem, both here in the UK and globally. In the UK, in 2017, around 7.33 million people were taking antidepressants. (9) I wonder what percentage of those were drinking at dangerous levels to alleviate the symptoms of poor mental health?

Depression can range in its intensity from mild, moderate through to severe. It can be caused by a range of social, psychological, and biological issues, too. Like problem drinking, it can be triggered by a life event, but it can also occur for no obvious reason whatsoever.

You could argue that depression is an over-used word, and how it feels can be a lot worse than it sounds. Symptoms can include a persistent low mood or sense of impending doom, constantly feeling tired, changes in appetite, irritability, disturbed sleep, and poor concentration. In addition, it is common to experience a lack of interest in activities that were previously enjoyable, plus a feeling of emptiness and hopelessness. They sound to me suspiciously like the symptoms of drinking too much.

Get help

This raises the question, what if you're suffering from alcohol dependence as well as depression? Which should you try to treat first? Obviously, the best place to start would be your doctor who will hopefully provide the support you need. Depression is treatable, as is problem drinking, though for some inexplicable reason, people feel more comfortable talking about depression than drinking, which is odd because statistically speaking, your doctor is likely to have just as much of a problem with the drink as you do.

Another vitally important reason to ensure that you discuss depression with your doctor is the potential risk of suicide. Globally around 800,000 people a year take their own life, and many more attempt to. It is thought that around half the people who commit suicide have been drinking before they do so. People who are drinking at dangerous levels are at eight times greater risk of suicide because as you know, alcohol can lower inhibitions. While women are at greater risk of suffering from depression, men are at a higher risk of suicide and are more likely to turn to alcohol if they are depressed.

Anxiety

Another reason people end up drinking too much is to try and cope with the symptoms of stress and anxiety. There are a wide range of anxiety disorders from a general anxiety disorder, post-traumatic stress disorder and social anxiety to name but a few. A certain amount of anxiety is good for us and is a natural reaction to a stressful situation, however, if you have ever experienced a panic attack, you will know that it does not feel like that at the time. Like depression, anxiety can also vary in its intensity.

Symptoms of anxiety can include feelings of worry and dread, a racing heart, shaking and trembling, lack of concentration, irritability, disturbed sleep, and changes in appetite. You can suffer from more than one anxiety disorder at once and you can experience anxiety and depression at the same time. (10)

I do wonder why, if we become physically or psychologically dependent on alcohol, that complete abstinence is sold as our only option. Abstinence isn't the only model, and the assumption that it is, suggests that we will only ever be passive victims. It implies that we will never be able to take control. As I have already explained, going from drinking a lot to being abstinent forever was unachievable for me. What I really wanted to do, although I couldn't articulate it clearly at the time, was to be better at moderating my drinking.

A better life

What is certain is that nobody regrets drinking less, or nobody that I know at least. I do not know one person, not one, who has ever regretted giving up drinking. Many people, I'm sure, use moderation as a stepping-stone to abstaining completely. Some people might miss it every now and again, but nobody regrets it. In fact, quite the opposite.

It is harder to find people who rave about learning to moderate their drinking, because it doesn't sound as dramatic or impressive as complete abstinence, but I do know some. I think the point I am trying to make is, however challenging or time-consuming it might be, it is worth continuing to analyse how much you are drinking, and why.

Lesley Miller & Catheryn Kell-Clarke

Some History of Alcohol in the United Kingdom

Cate

'Wine is sunlight, held together by water.'

~ Galileo

As you know by now, I adore the UK, so it made perfect sense to me to look more deeply into its history with alcohol. In this chapter, I have stuck to the information that I found the most fascinating. It is impossible to share all the information and again, I would encourage you to do a bit of research of your own. I was particularly interested in discovering how gin, as you know, a favourite tipple of mine, made it to England's shores and became such a favourite. This seemed like a great place to start.

Gin flows in old London town

A book I found to be an incredibly interesting read was, Mark Forsyth's, *A Short History of Drunkenness* (2017). In it, he mentions that London was the place to be, back in the 1700s. Some of the reasons for this were, that it was said that the streets were paved with gold, fortunes were to be made and anything was possible. The population back then was around 600,000, not a lot by today's numbers but back then, very few towns in England had populations over 20,000. (1)

In the late 1700s, gin was very popular, just as it is today. (2) You may have seen old images of crowded street scenes with mothers swigging gin and grubby, unkempt children around their feet. Forsyth suggested that gin became popular in England for four reasons; the monarchy, the army, religion and an end to world hunger. He also proposed that a fifth reason was a possibility, that of the hatred of the French. (3) You see, the Brits were staunch enemies of France and many wars were waged between these two countries. France's strict Catholic views and the absolute power of Louis XIV also caused much fear and hatred.

In 1689, King William III, or William of Orange, became King of England, Ireland, and Scotland and he was the monarch until his death in 1702. He began his reign by implementing trade wars and protectionist-style economic tactics against France. Blockades and heavy taxes on French wine and Cognac were introduced to weaken the French economy. Now he also liked gin, he was Dutch after all, and as everyone knew back then, nearly all Dutch people liked to drink gin. Gin became the drink to be drinking by the then well-to-do. (4)

Dutch Courage

Back then, European countries were frequently at war with one another, and these disputes were often over religion. England and Holland were both Protestant countries and so they often fought together. When fighting one of these many wars alongside the Dutch, the English soldiers noticed how brave and fearless they were. Gin, it seemed, made Dutch soldiers particularly brave. You've heard of 'Dutch Courage'? Now you know where the term comes from. The English and Dutch would often drink gin together and upon returning home after the wars, the English soldiers brought the taste for gin back with them and they continued to consume it. (5)

Another reason for the popularity of gin, suggested by Forsyth (2017), was that of ending world hunger. In a good year, the farmers would produce enough grain to feed everybody, no more, no less. If too much was produced in any given year, they would have difficulty in selling it. When there was a bad harvest, this was, believe it or not, good for the farmers as a shortage of grain meant they could charge higher prices. Clearly a lack of food wasn't great for anyone else, however. (6)

Enter King William III, who by many accounts, was an unremarkable, and a not particularly handsome man. He did, however, have a plan and thought he knew how to solve the problem. You guessed it - gin! (7)

The plan - booze not bread

Now, as you may know, gin is made out of grain. Whether the grain was of good or bad quality did not matter much, for once it is distilled, the difference in taste is negligible. If gin could be made popular in England, William believed this would enable him to create a demand for any surplus grain that was produced during a normal year. The result would be that in a bad harvest season, the surplus from a normal year would cover the shortfall, and people could still be fed. Genius! But, to make this plan work, gin had to become popular.

Now how did he go about this? William decided to make gin more widely available and easier to access than beer. It was unregulated and entirely tax-free. Anyone who wished to could set up a gin shop. The result was that gin was everywhere and it was available from all kinds of places; from shops to workhouses, prisons and madhouses. It was also sold from wheelbarrows, down alleys and from back rooms in cheap lodging houses. (8)

The raw spirit for the gin was bought from the large malt distillers and it was distilled a second time. This second distillation resulted in almost doubling its potency, to around 80 per cent which is almost twice that of today's gins. As well as juniper for flavouring, the likes of turpentine and sulphuric acid could also be added. Yuck!

Mother's Ruin

All was good. Or so you would have thought. However, along with the wealth, there was also incredible destitution. The slums in the East End and around Westminster were where these unfortunates tended to congregate. Here they sought to forget the villages, and the better lifestyle they had left behind. Enter gin; cheap, strong and plentiful to dull their painful memories. (9)

Significant amounts of this cheap gin were drunk and as a result, many deaths occurred. Not surprising really when you consider how strong it was. Now you might ask, was there any stigma to drinking so much? I wondered this also and well, no, there wasn't. The growing urban poor in London needed relief from their problems, and the research suggests that women weren't judged for neglecting their children and taking to the gin. You may have heard of gin described as 'Mother's Ruin'? (10)

The so-called Gin Epidemic was at its height and the amount of drinking and debauchery that was occurring became concerning for those who were meant to be in control of society, the upper classes. To try and quell the many resulting issues, numerous gin acts were passed by the government, most famously in 1736 & 1751.

These acts taxed and regulated the production and sale of gin and prohibited its sale in quantities of less than two gallons. Figures from that time are fascinating. Apparently at its peak, in 1743 the consumption of gin in a nation of six and a half million people was over 18 million gallons! By 1758, that was down to just two million gallons, although this still sounds like a lot to me. Gin began to lose its popularity as beer was now being sold at a lower price, and coffee was also becoming more popular.

Piety increased amongst the population and gin fell out of favour. Furthermore, the new industrial age valued sobriety, as drunkenness around large machinery was considered dangerous and frowned upon. Quite rightly. (11)

Drinking in Victorian and Edwardian Britain

During the late 1820s and the early 1830s, developments in the manufacturing of the brewing stills saw the creation of the famous London Dry gins. I was interested to learn that London Dry does not in fact mean that the gin is made in London. It could be made anywhere and it refers instead to how it is made rather than the location. There are some gins which do have a geographical indication, 13 of them in fact.

In our pub, we sold the most well-known, that of Plymouth Gin, which had been made since 1793 in, no prizes for guessing, Plymouth, England. To produce London Dry, the base spirit must be distilled to a completely neutral spirit of 9 per cent alcoholic volume. All the flavours are to be sourced from natural plant materials and they must be added through the distillation. Nothing may be added after distillation, except for water and a small amount of sugar. (12)

Also, around this time, gin and tonic water became acquainted. In British colonies such as India and in South East Asia where malaria was prevalent, gin was used to disguise the flavour of quinine which had a particularly bitter taste. Quinine, which was an effective anti-malarial compound, was dissolved in carbonated water and became known as tonic water. The resulting cocktail, a gin and tonic, was born. And yes, in case you are wondering, I did drink G & T's when I lived in Singapore. You can't be too careful around mosquitoes. Today's tonic water, however, contains only a trace of quinine, probably not really enough to deter those pesky mozzies. (13)

The Teetotal and Temperance movements

Another aspect that intrigued me from around this time was that of both the Temperance and Teetotal movements. These were most popular in the 1830s and 1840s. You may have heard of them? The **Teetotal Movement** came about from those who fervently believed in the evil of alcohol. They called for an alcohol-free society and formed a group, the 'Teetotaller's.' This group tried to persuade those who would listen that consuming alcohol was morally wrong. Leaders of the Teetotal Movement were more working class, and they had links with Chartism, a working-class political movement which sought better social and industrial conditions for the working classes. Chartism favoured complete abstention from alcohol. (14)

Teetotalism was a reaction against what was viewed as the hypocrisy of arguments for moderation and the middle-classes support of alcohol, also known as the **Temperance Movement.** The Temperance movement were opposed to spirits but advocated the moderate use of beer. Their main goal was not to outlaw drinking, but to control it. Many working-class men, however, were insulted by this movement and believed that its bourgeois leaders were hypocritical because they implied that the problem of drunkenness lay only with the working class. The consumption of alcohol among working-class men began to be viewed as a wasteful and illicit form of entertainment which served no purpose and caused many problems. Whereas wine, the favoured drink of the middle-class was seen as acceptable. This was scorned and fought against by the Temperance Movement.

The idea behind the Temperance Movement was managing the unruly working class and was led by middle-class social reformers and philanthropists. This movement tried to convince the working class that spending their wages on clothes, food, and middle-class comforts was a better option rather than wasting it on beer or spirits. The movement recommended the introduction of more productive leisure and social activities. It sought to provide libraries and lectures to fill working men's free time. The Temperance Movement continued well into the twentieth century. This leads me to question whether the idea of temperance was any more achievable back then than it is for some of us now. (15, 16)

Alcohol and medicine

Learning about the use of alcohol in medical practice was also fascinating. It was used from the seventeenth century and became increasingly popular in the nineteenth century. (17)

By the late nineteenth century, however, some doctors had stopped prescribing alcohol and much debate about its therapeutic value raged. The question of whether it actually did more harm than good was a hot topic, and as you know, remains so today. Doctors, it seemed, could not agree on what 'healthy' amounts of alcohol consumption were or if alcohol was in fact beneficial. It seems that even today this is still a complex issue.

In a presidential address to the British Society for the Study of Inebriety in July 1907, Dr. Harry Campbell discussed the influence of alcohol on health, and asked what a moderate use of alcohol would be:

".... is moderate indulgence the equivalent of one, two, three, or four glasses of whisky per diem? ... I recently asked a casual acquaintance what he understood by moderate and he gave as an answer, "half a bottle of whisky a day." And I told him that I was going to suggest two glasses, or their equivalent to which he replied that a man who limited himself to so small a quantity was to all intents and purposes a teetotaller!"

We've all had these conversations. How much is too much? Campbell concluded that by failing to quantify what moderate drinking was and the type of alcohol that should be drunk, the authors of the article had not done their job. He believed that the quality and type of alcohol were key factors in determining its effects on someone's health. We know now that there really is no safe limit regardless of these factors. (18)

Alcohol and the First World War

Hospital records show that although the use of alcohol had diminished in the period leading up to the First World War, doctors still relied on it to treat a range of physiological and psychological illnesses. During the war, people seemed to believe that moderate consumption was desirable as it improved the nation's fighting spirit and helped to preserve morale. Alcohol, boosted peoples' self-confidence and increased their willingness to take risks. Inebriated soldiers felt invincible and would be more confident to take greater risks. By consuming alcohol, they would more readily go over the top of the trenches and run towards the enemy fire. Remember 'Dutch Courage'? Drinking was also thought to strengthen the bonds and built trust, which was seen as vital for group unity. Alcohol, it was thought, also helped to repress traumatic memories and supported people to cope with the horrors of war. (19)

In early 1915, the then Prime Minister of Great Britain, Lloyd George, said:

'...fighting Germans, Austrians and drink, and as far as I can see the greatest of these foes is drink.' (20)

He started a campaign to persuade national figures to make a pledge that they would not drink alcohol during the war. King George V supported his campaign and in April 1915, promised that alcohol would not be consumed in the Royal household until the war was over. Later that year, the British government introduced new measures to help reduce alcohol consumption. (21)

The new measures

A 'No Treating Order' is what it says on the label. Any drink that was ordered had to be paid for by the person it was given to. It was essentially a 'you pay-you drink' law, where you couldn't buy someone else a drink.

Every man, and woman for themself. The maximum penalty for defying this law was six months' imprisonment. The hours pubs could open in cities and industrial areas were also reduced. These new hours were from noon until 2.30 pm and then from 6 pm until 9.30 pm. Previously, pubs could be open from 5 am until 12.30 am the following morning, if the landlord desired. Pity the poor bar staff! These new measures did see a slight reduction in drinking during this time and these measures lasted until the depression of the early 1930s. (22)

So, very briefly, these were some of the facts I found fascinating about alcohol and its history in the UK.

Alcohol Reconsidered

The Marketing of Alcohol

Cate

'There are only two real ways to get ahead today - sell liquor or drink it.'

~ W. C. Fields

The alcohol industry exists to make money. Whilst you might not think too much about what drink you have in your hand or why, be assured that once you were of legal drinking age, you became a target for the marketing companies. If you want further evidence, just think about the wine culture of today. It didn't exist like it does today 30 years ago, and that was because the marketers of the time hadn't realised that there was a group, they had not targeted yet, women.

Through I've had some experience of selling alcohol myself, looking at this chapter made me more aware of the exceptionally skilful ways that the marketing companies influence our choices.

The importance of cool

One particular example I remember clearly, was when I was first working in London. There was great excitement amongst the bar staff when we were 'given' a Budweiser bar fridge. I use inverted commas when I say we were given because, of course, it wasn't really free. We were all expected to sell and promote Budweiser over the real ales. I had assumed that this would be a tricky task as our regulars were generally young, pint drinking lads from the surrounding banks or the hospitality crews from the nearby gentlemen's clubs who were partial to a glass of wine or two. A bottle of Budweiser wasn't their usual tipple of choice nor did they seem to be the types who worried about looking cool. But much to my surprise, we sold Budweiser and a lot of it. That 'free' fridge seemed to do the trick, and the customers switched from their usual drink choices to bottles of Bud. It became cool, whether male or female to have a bottle to swig from. Drink industries now target a younger audience through alcopops, which are sweet and sugary knowing that in time they will progress onto harder liquor. Being 'cool' has it seems, always been important.

The personal touch

I also learnt back then, that I could easily recommend a drink and make a sale. It was all in the pitch, the banter, the chat. I tended to push the Australian wines, mainly because New Zealand hadn't really begun to make their mark on the wine world yet. *'A glass of 'sunshine-in-a-bottle' anyone?'* I was in an exciting position with a wide range of drink choices to suggest to the customers.

My point is, that word of mouth proved to me to be an extremely valuable marketing tool just as it is today. But what if there is no enthusiastic Kiwi in your pub or bar to suggest what to drink? Where do your ideas come from? Are you influenced by the marketing companies or do you rely on recommendations from friends?

Offers & promotions

Before trying to answer my questions, let's look at some of the methods the companies use to market a product. And let's be honest here, people generally want to make the purchase in the first place. Why therefore are millions being spent on advertising?

When we ran the pub, we preferred to rely on word of mouth, positive reviews on social media, and our pub's prominent location in the village. We were content to let the brewery do all the hard work for us with their seasonal beer offers, the beer pump badges and posters advertising the latest brew. We had plenty of customers, often more than we could easily cope with, so there was no real need for us to have 'Thirsty Thursdays', 'Fizzy Fridays' or promote the buy two large glasses of wine and have the rest of the bottle for free. I wonder, did you know that the last promotion, is deemed to be an irresponsible sale of alcohol? This is something every landlord knows, yet this type of promotion continues in many pubs and restaurants. (1)

Another snippet I learnt while I was wearing my landlady's hat was that it is a legal requirement to offer wine in 125ml glasses. To run a pub, you need to have a personal licence, which is an odd name, I've always thought for something required to sell alcohol. Part of the legal understanding is that a 125ml glass must be made available. Think back to the last glass of wine you were ordered, *'Would you like a medium or large Pinot madam?'* I'd suggest that very rarely will you be offered a small one. I wonder, did the bar even have small wine glasses on display? (2, 3)

What is advertising?

As any teacher knows, if the student in their class doesn't know the meaning of the word, what do you get them to do? Tell them to look it up in the dictionary of course. Every classroom I ever worked in seemed to have at least 40 dictionaries, all sitting neatly on a dusty shelf. They're probably quite redundant now in these technologically savvy times. In the spirit of the age, I consulted WordHippo.com which listed other words for 'advertise'. The list included:

Promote, declare, flaunt, flog, peddle, proclaim, publish, advance, announce. (4)

Gosh, not all that complementary. I particularly loved 'flog' and 'flaunt'. Essentially the nuts and bolts of it, that's what advertising is and it really is a big business.

The basics of marketing

The basics of marketing boil down to ideas known in the marketing trade as the **4Ps**. This terminology became popular in the fifties and is still used today.

They are:

The **product,** essentially, what you are selling. In this case, alcohol.

The **price,** the consumer will pay for the goods. Considerations such as a fair monetary value, supply costs and competitors' pricing need to be factored in when attaching a value to a product. Prosecco or Champagne? Which one are you prepared to pay more for? A product which is more difficult and expensive to manufacture?

The **place** where your product will be sold. Will it be sold in a store? Online? At the supermarket? Or at the local pub?

The **promotion** of your product or service. What marketing strategy will be used to present your product or service? Could it be a sale with flyers and posters created to promote it? Perhaps the product could be advertised through the media, either social or in print? (5)

The marketing of alcohol

Now the marketing of alcohol has changed over the years. One reason for this change could be because our view of alcohol has altered. Professor Nutt (2020), claims that the way we consume alcohol has changed over the past 50 years. He contends that in the past, alcohol was a special purchase. Historically, here in the UK and in other countries, you had to go to an off-license or to the pub during limited hours to buy your drinks. From the seventies, however, governments around the world liberalised the way people purchased alcohol. Increasing the hours in which they could do this was also introduced. Nutt suggests, and we agree with him, that we now have a tendency to buy alcohol as part of our weekly shop. We pop it into our trolley alongside the carrots and broccoli with no real thought. Or perhaps we wait for the man in the van to deliver to our door? Think back to when you were younger. What were the laws and rules about buying alcohol back then? What can you remember? Where did you buy your last drink? (6)

Alcohol advertising trends

The first advertising in the UK, it may be said, was on the dray, the horse and carts used to transport the beer from the brewery to the pubs. Company names and later logos were painted onto the side or above the driving seat on the cart. The dray is still around today, albeit in lorry form. Breweries' logos and well-known beer brands can be seen displayed across these delivery trucks around the country. When we had the pub, our beer delivery day was on a Wednesday and when the shout, 'the dray's here!' went out, I would frequently rush to take a photograph of it or the ensuing delivery to post on our Facebook page. I was declaring to the locals that the alcohol had arrived, just like the breweries would have done back in their brief newspaper notices in the nineteenth century. We could all breathe a sigh of relief.

The abolition of advertising duty occurred in 1853 here in the UK. This meant that brewers could now advertise their products. Up until this point, breweries could only promote where their beer could be drunk rather than the beer itself. A few sparse lines would be found in newspapers stating the brewing cycle had been completed, and the beer was ready to drink. It seems brewers in the nineteenth century, did very little to promote their products.

After the advertising duty had been lifted, these brief lines became more descriptive and fantastic, although it was still more likely that one would hear about the availability of a new brew by word of mouth. Remember at this time the water supplies were often hazardous and while spirits were deemed to be harmful, beer was viewed as a healthy and nutritious choice. In fact, the Temperance Movement promoted beer for its health-giving qualities. Historians believe these brief lines were intended for the information of the public rather than as advertisement. It seems that most English brewers believed a good product was their best form of advertising. (7)

In 1875, a Trade Marks Act was introduced. This meant alcohol could be promoted with companies using recognisable images. The first to capitalise on these new laws were Bass and Guinness. You may still recognise the catchphrases they used back then. Slogans began appearing on posters and signs, clocks, calendars, and many other items. I'm sure everyone could recognise a slogan or two. They're what sticks in your mind long after the drink has gone. Think about, *'Carlsberg... Probably the best beer in the world',* a very well-known slogan or perhaps *'I bet he drinks Carling Black Label.'* Then there was *'I'd love a Babycham.' (8, 9)*

In the early twentieth century, the idea of promoting alcohol for health may explain why early advertising tended to focus on 'lifestyle' advertising. Advertisements associating alcohol products with middle-class sporting activities like golf and cricket were to be seen. The beer duty was increased in the thirties and this led to a decline in consumption. This, in turn, resulted in an increase in advertising.

The cost of advertising alcohol

The amount alcoholic beverage companies spend on advertising is simply phenomenal. They shell out between $1 and $2 billion each year on print and broadcast media adverts alone. Anheuser-Busch Co., the Budweiser fridge guys, spent $US1.53 billion on advertising in America in 2019. This money also includes other alcohol-related advertising and promotional programs such as rock concerts and activities, usually on university or college campuses. Think back to when you were at university. Was there a sponsor for your Fresher's Week drinks? What drinks were at a discounted rate? I talked about my university town being awash with alcohol. Now you know why. There's big money to be made, even from poor students. (10)

Sponsorship

Sports teams often have an alcohol brand associated with them and, more likely than not, as one of their main sponsors. But marketing is expensive, and the sponsorship of sports is big bucks too. Over $US760 million is spent each year by the 30 leading alcoholic beverage brands, sponsorship of competitions, teams and athletes in the industry making up most of the cost. (11)

This led me to the question, why all the bother? What's in it for the alcohol companies? Conrad Wiacek, the Head of Sponsorship at Sportcal states that it all comes down to reaching the target audience, often the older males, who, he suggests, don't respond strongly to traditional advertising. The alcohol companies' pair with the teams and athletes, and share the success or failures, thereby making themselves part of the conversation and in turn, building loyalty amongst fans. Sportcal estimates that Guinness, which is owned by Diageo, the multinational drinks conglomerate, spent more than $10 million as the headline sponsor of Six Nations Rugby during the 2020 season. Like I said, big bucks. I wonder do males drink more than females at sporting events or are, perhaps, women giving them a run for their money? (12)

My favourite rugby team, the All Blacks, have Steinlager, a rather tasty New Zealand-made lager as one of their sponsors. They have been together since 1986. That's a long time in anyone's books. Did I rush out and buy a six-pack of 'Steinies' to drink while I watched the game? Did I order a Steinlager at the pub? Well yes, you bet I did, because I also wanted to feel like part of the team. My other favourite rugby team, the Highlanders from Otago, also have a brewery as their sponsor, Speights, from Dunedin. They've been a part of the team since 1996, again quite some time. (13, 14)

I wonder how much money has been spent by Steinlager and Speights over those years. I also wonder how many sports teams' supporters have been influenced by what their team's jersey or the bar at the stadium was promoting. The product had exclusivity and the 'I'm special' appeal.

Globally, alcohol and sport are seen to go together. In fact, the two have been in partnership since the sixteenth century. Back then, the local pub would often be the venue for things like skittles or quoits, bowls, wrestling, tennis, and cricket. It was also the place for events involving animals, such as cock fighting. (15)

Pink drinks

As you may have detected from the content of this chapter so far, historically, the drinks industry aimed their efforts at men. Over the time though, someone spotted a gap in the market and women began to be the target.

As I've already pointed out, the drinks industry is very clever. They have spent a lot of time and money designing products that will appeal to both sexes and the range for women is ever increasing. From fruity ciders and beers, to essentially anything pink with bubbles, we certainly can't say that they haven't thought about us.

The industry has also cottoned onto the fact that women weren't that keen on being defined as passive sex objects, so they have upped their game. Advertising aimed at women is now likely to tap into our desires to be empowered and you will often see images of women with their friends, 'the sisterhood' in an attempt for us to identify with. I'm sure we are all familiar with phrases such as 'wine o'clock' or 'mummy's little helper' that are all designed to make us feel like we deserve a drink and are often linked to so-called, 'me time'.

Some companies, I'd argue, have gone too far. There is something quite insidious about brand names such as 'skinny girl vodka', presumably trying to cash in on our insecurities about how we look. The BrewDog brewery produced an IPA called 'Trashy Blonde'. I wonder who they were targeting with this ale. They have since had a change of heart about it and it is now no longer on the market. Arguably even more disingenuous attempts to market drinks to us has come in the form of support for 'International Women's Day', or to highlight the gender pay gap. If you keep your ears open, you might hear the words that are increasingly used to get us to link alcoholic drinks with our lifestyles. If you hear the word 'botanical' in an advertisement or see celebrities on TV discussing their organically produced, clean wines, pay attention. This is referred to by some as 'commodity feminism'. (16)

We can all fall for the market tricks that these companies use, so they are worth paying attention to and thinking about which of the 4P's the industry is using to draw you into purchasing, because be very clear, they aren't really all that concerned about your 'you time' or your health.

Who is responsible?

In 1962, the Advertising Standards Authority was established here, and various codes of practice were introduced. This meant the more dubious examples of alcohol advertising were banned. In the past, these advertisements thought nothing of using sexist, racist language or just downright incorrect information to present the product to their willing public.

Over the years, there has also been concern that children have been exposed to too many alcohol advertisements, although the number broadcast in the UK has dropped dramatically in recent years. I wonder though, is it enough?

In 2008, the Labour government introduced laws to restrict price promotions and ran 'responsible drinking' campaigns to allay public concerns regarding alcohol marketing and binge-drinking. Despite the health select committee in 2010 calling for a watershed, where no advertising would be shown prior to 9 pm, no changes to the alcohol advertising rules for TV were made. However, after much lobbying by various sources, the number of advertisements on TV has decreased dramatically. In 2019, less than one per cent of television ads seen by children featured alcohol. (17)

Social media is now used to promote alcohol and drinking venues so there is clearly still work to be done to protect the vulnerable. The ongoing debate regarding the self-regulation of the industry continues, both here in the UK and globally. The reduction of alcohol in television advertising, seen by children, seems to be, thankfully, a global phenomenon. When was the last time you saw an advertisement for alcohol on the TV? You're more likely to see advertisements for alcohol on your social media feeds. (18)

Social media and alcohol companies

Social media plays a huge part in the promotion of alcohol. Drink companies are willing to shell out vast amounts of money on social media platforms to promote their products. Previously, Lesley and I had believed that social media could be viewed as an informal type of advertising, yet delving more deeply into the marketing of alcohol, I now see this assumption was incorrect.

Social media tends to only portray the fun, glamourous side of drinking and very rarely shares the hangovers the following morning. It's more often than not, a post of the big night out itself rather than the morning after. I'll bet the last photo you added on your social media was of you looking gorgeous with maybe a glass of fizz in your hand, or perhaps you tweeted about the delicious Pinot you'd just ordered? Odds are it wasn't the day after the night before, of you looking and feeling rough. We are, whenever we tweet or post or comment, telling the world what we like to drink and how much fun it is helping us to have. I believe that the alcohol companies are also doing that. They are invertedly asking us to buy into the illusion that alcohol is needed for fun, a good time, to make an event a celebration.

Research conducted in 2012 by the School of Humanities and Cultural Industries in Bath, analysed social media and found clear patterns in the strategies used when marketing alcohol.

The most common was the use of so-called **real-world tie-ins.** This is where events such as club nights or sporting events were promoted on social media and techniques such as interactive games, sponsored online events and invitations to drink were used. Remember this was over eight years ago so I would suspect that given the growth in social media platforms over the past few years, these strategies will have increased dramatically. By using social media, the companies aimed to begin conversations about alcohol. It also provided marketers access to the profile data of users who clicked the 'like' button on the pages.

The research also found that **surveys and quizzes** were common on Facebook, particularly with wine brands and these received a large number of posts. The giveaways and competitions promoted could be entered by participants with no purchase necessary. Think about the number of times you've been pulled into a quiz or survey on Facebook.

Encouragement to drink posts were also found to regularly appear. These were often day-specific, that is connected perhaps to the weekend or early and mid-week consumption. The most common posts were found to be on a Friday, as well as 'Mojito Monday' or Wednesday, 'hump day'. Phrases such as 'Raise your glass to the start of the weekend', or 'Sunday's fun day', were posted in real-time.

This research found that **responsible drinking promotion** was not done a great deal and that few Facebook posts explicitly recommended moderate or responsible drinking. I would suggest that this is not particularly surprising given the main purpose of marketing is to make money. (19, 20)

WKD, an alcopop and Foster's beer were the only brands at the time found to promote responsible drinking as they included a permanent message with a live link to the Drinkaware website on their wall or launch page. **Drinkaware** is an independent UK-wide alcohol education charity and it was previously the responsibility of the Portman group, which was made up of alcoholic beverage producers and brewers in the UK. Drinkaware is funded mainly by voluntary and unrestricted donations from UK alcohol producers, retailers and supermarkets. (21)

'House rules' were found on some brands pages. Rules such as those against depicting under 25-year-olds in photographs while others provided a link to Drinkaware on their separate 'about' pages. The researchers found that permanent links to responsible drinking guidelines or resources were notable by their absence on most of the Facebook walls.

As this research was conducted over eight years ago, I wondered had this changed? Having looked at various drink pages on Facebook recently, it seemed to show me that it had. However, in saying that, only about 50 per cent of the pages I visited had any kind of responsible drinking message. I would suggest that there is still room for improvement.

We need to ask ourselves, are we all being very subtly brainwashed every time we check our social media feeds?

Who funds the research?

Something I hadn't really considered until I was writing this chapter was the issue of industry funding. In 2018, Public Health England (PHE), wanted to develop an advertising campaign promoting the idea that people should have at least two alcohol-free days a week. There was no money available - where have we heard that before? - so they agreed to partner up with Drinkaware. This upset hundreds of academics who signed a petition censoring PHE and resulted in Ian Gilmore, PHE's senior alcohol advisor resigning in protest. (22)

The content of the campaign wasn't what was particularly contentious, rather it was where the money was coming from. Professor Nutt had no real issue with the industry funding independent research and education, on the proviso that they didn't have any influence on its content. Long story short, the campaign didn't happen and as a result, Professor Nutt suggests, people have died from not knowing this information. This I found absolutely shocking, and something I'll lay wager many people don't know about. (23)

So many questions in this one chapter. I wonder, are you influenced by the advertising companies? Did you, for example, buy that bottle of Irish Cream Liqueur at Christmas time because you automatically associate Christmas with this drink? Was alcohol advertising really necessary during the Covid-19 crisis? Did people locked down at home really need to be told what to consume? I wonder, did companies continue to spend vast amounts of money during the pandemic or did they reduce the spend? I suspect in the months to come we may just find out the answers to some of these questions.

Lesley Miller & Catheryn Kell-Clarke

The Impact of Alcohol

Lesley

'Drunkenness is nothing but voluntary madness.'

~ Seneca

When I first started putting alcohol under the microscope, I was really looking at drinking from my own perspective. At that point, I hadn't spent much time considering the scale of the problems that alcohol creates for society as a whole.

Some of the things I discovered when I conducted my research were genuinely shocking, and at times, I wondered if it wasn't morally reprehensible to sell alcohol at all. We will explore why that is a more complicated solution than it initially seems, in the next chapter, but for now, let's just consider what some of the issues are. For this chapter, I have mainly looked at statistics in the UK, but there are similar trends in many other countries.

Millennials and Generation Z drinking less

At a first glance, the statistics on our consumption in the UK appear to look quite positive. They show that alcohol consumption is declining overall. While this may be true, it doesn't give us the full picture. The younger generations seem to be turning their back on alcohol and there appears to have been a cultural shift in this age group. (1) It is increasingly common for people to identify as being 'sober curious' and no doubt campaigns such as 'Stoptober' and 'Dry January' are making the options of moderation or complete abstinence more visible and socially acceptable.

Perhaps younger people are more educated about the ills of alcohol? Maybe they are more committed to a healthier lifestyle, or maybe there's a financial element influencing their lifestyle choices too? It costs around £8, and often more, for a large glass of wine in London, which by anyone's standards is a lot. I certainly wouldn't have been able to drink at those prices when I was younger.

There is, in fact, a range of evidence from several countries suggesting that minimum pricing is an effective strategy for reducing alcohol sales which we will come to shortly. As you might expect, 'minimum pricing' is when alcohol can't be sold for less than a certain price per unit.

Older drinkers

It is the 'baby boomers', those aged between 55 and 64 who are more likely to drink the most heavily, and are the least likely demographic to abstain from alcohol. In fact, abstinence rates have declined in the over 65 age group. (2) The reasons why are just as complicated as everything else to do with alcohol. Every generation has its challenges and perhaps it's the changes that occur in later life that are contributory factors. We've already explored the reasons why people drink, and when you consider that older age can bring with it changing roles in the workplace, retirement, more money and time, loneliness, along with health issues, maybe it isn't any wonder.

Men at more risk

As we've mentioned several times, men are more likely to be drinkers than women. Since records began in 2001, rates of death from alcohol-related illnesses have consistently doubled for men when compared to women. The majority of these deaths are through alcoholic liver disease. It is worth pointing out though, that the number of women being admitted to hospital with alcohol-related illness is increasing. (3) I find this interesting because when I talk to my female friends, it is often their husbands and partners who are getting increasingly worried about my friends' drinking, and not the other way around. But we need to ask, why is alcohol consumption affecting men so disproportionately, and why isn't more being done about it? And why are older women drinking more? I'd argue that these questions need publicly exploring in greater depth.

Alcohol & public health

When we think about society, we should, perhaps, begin with the impact alcohol has on public health. NHS Digital, a provider of health-related statistics in the UK, shows that between 2018 and 2019, in England alone, there were approximately 358,000 hospital admissions as a result of alcohol consumption. That is a 19 per cent increase since the period between 2008 and 2009. (4) It is statistics like these that illustrate why we should be cautious about reports that claim that we are drinking less as they may over-simplify the progress being made.

I expect you may not be the sort of drinker who ends up in a hospital, although if you haven't yourself, you might know someone who has at some point. I remember nearly breaking my ankle the night before my sister's wedding many years ago, as I'd gone out to a nightclub with a friend and he rather too enthusiastically spun me around when we were dancing. Or maybe I was dancing too energetically? I can't remember. This resulted in me falling over on my ankle and so I ended up in Accident and Emergency which was full of other young people who were also drunk.

There was another time when I was under the influence that I fell onto some broken glass in what turned out to be an unnecessary attempt to get rid of a wasp from my flat. It isn't an exaggeration to say I'm petrified of wasps, so I put a glass over the top of it and a piece of card underneath, you get the idea. I shakily managed a few steps, then tripped on the balcony. The glass smashed just before I fell onto it, and the result was that I sliced my hand open. This required another trip to the hospital. I still have the scar on my palm now, and this was all unnecessary as the wasp was, as it turned out, dead anyway.

Injuring myself whilst drinking wasn't anything unusual when I was younger. Neither were the fights and arguments.

Cost to the NHS

It is estimated that the cost of alcohol to the NHS is a whopping £3.5 billion a year, and around 80 people a day die from alcohol-related injuries. It is thought that a tenth of all patients in hospital beds are alcohol dependent. I think we can all agree that is a staggering statistic. (5) When you consider the scale of the problem, it really doesn't seem to make sense that there have been so many cuts to alcohol support services over the years. You would have thought that if people were given the right support, this would in fact save the government money in the longer term.

Accidents & injuries

Even if you don't drink to the point where you break your bones, you may be familiar with random bruising. Because of the anaesthetic qualities of alcohol, we often don't feel it when we injure ourselves, or even remember how it happened. We know how alcohol affects our brains and behaviour, so it doesn't require any leap of the imagination to see why binge drinking can lead to all sorts of health issues and accidents. One of the major problems with alcohol is that some of the negative consequences don't just affect us. This is why it is considered by some experts to be the most damaging drug of them all - not just because of the damage it does to us individually, but because of the harm we can cause others.

Road traffic accidents

In 2018, 8,700 people in the UK were injured or killed in road accidents where alcohol had been involved. Around 250 people die every year in the UK as a result of drink-driving accidents. (6) The UK isn't the only country that grapples with the problem of drink driving and the statistics for road fatalities caused by alcohol are high in other countries such as South Africa, America, Canada and Australia to name but a few. (7)

Drink driving doesn't just affect us mere mortals either. Do you remember the tragedy of the deaths of Princess Diana, Dodi Fayed and Henri Paul back in August 1997? It is alleged that Henri Paul, who was driving the car, was over the limit at the time.

It's not just the drink drivers that contribute to these statistics. There are also drunk pedestrians and cyclists who get hit and injured because their judgement is impaired. One of my friends in my younger days hit a cyclist with his car and killed him. It wasn't my friend's error that caused the accident. It was the cyclist who had made an error of judgement, possibly because he was three times over the limit. However much we tried to reassure him that it was a tragic accident and that it wasn't his fault, he still felt an overwhelming sense of guilt. It took him months to get back in his car and he suffered very badly from depression and anxiety. Drink driving has been the focus of many campaigns and the problem used to be much worse than it is now.

Domestic abuse

It isn't just the NHS that alcohol has an impact on either. The police spend around £1 billion annually dealing with alcohol-related crime. (8) It is thought that a significant amount of violent crime involves alcohol, as you might expect. You might know yourself if you've ever had an argument with someone when either of you has been drinking that it can lead to you, or them, becoming more aggressive. Drinking can intensify our emotions. It's easy to misjudge situations and social cues, get the wrong end of the stick and draw the wrong conclusions.

There is also a well-established link between alcohol and domestic abuse. It is thought that in the UK, one in four women and one in six men will experience this type of abuse at some point during their lifetime. The figures in other countries are similar and it remains an issue across the world. That means that statistically speaking either you or someone that you know, will have experienced it. (9)

The effects domestic violence can have on its victims are devastating. It can lead to physical injuries and mental health issues. Two women a week and 30 men a year are killed by either their current or ex-partner in the UK. It goes without saying that if you are experiencing any form of domestic abuse, we would **very strongly** urge you to get the help and support you need.

Alcohol and children

Of course, alcoholism and violence don't just affect adults. Discovering the effect that alcohol can have on children makes for some pretty grim reading.

Around 200,000 children in the UK live with alcohol-dependent parents. This could very well be a gross underestimate because we know that people often underestimate how much alcohol they consume, and I expect the fear of having their children taken away from them prevents many people from seeking the help that they need. (10)

It is unbearable to think of children being damaged either physically or psychologically by their parents' drinking, but it is not unusual. I tried, unsuccessfully, to find out how many children were taken into care each year because of a parent's drinking. What I did find was plenty of stories of children who had disrupted bedtimes, poor attendance at school, and the burden of having to look after younger siblings. There are harrowing first-hand accounts of parents who had their children taken away from them. There were awful tales of abuse and neglect and even, as a 'problem drinker' myself, I found it hard not to be hypocritical or to judge people for not getting help.

Of course, people do not deserve mine or anyone else's judgement, what they need is help. And besides, when I took a cold, hard look at my own parenting skills, there was in the past, room for improvement.

Alcohol & lost income

Lost productivity and sick days from employees cost businesses around the world £7.3 billion a year. (11) I don't expect that I need to tell you what working with a hangover feels like. Employees who are heavy and moderate drinkers are also more likely to be a risk to themselves and others.

I can honestly say, with my hand on my heart, that I haven't ever pulled a sickie because of a hangover. My philosophy was that if I was stupid enough to drink too much, then I should suffer the consequences and show up for work. Employers have a responsibility for the wellbeing and health and safety of their staff, and they are encouraged to provide support where possible for someone who has a drinking problem. Of course, many people hide their drinking from their partners and their work colleagues.

In some cases, people drink because of the stress at their job. Interestingly, just over a quarter of people say that workplace stress makes them drink more, and that is a statistic that anyone can relate to, us included. Perhaps this goes some way to explaining why it is, that people in professional and managerial roles drink more than others. City workers, lawyers and high earning professionals are drinking the most, as are, ironically, medical professionals. A recent study published in the Occupational Medical Journal found that 45 per cent of Intensive Care workers have either turned to alcohol or had suicidal thoughts during the Covid-19 pandemic. (12)

So, all this does beg the question that if we know that drinking is creating such significant problems to individuals and society, what are we going to do about it? It is likely that if alcohol suddenly appeared on the market now it would be illegal as a foodstuff. Why isn't it being demonised and taxed to the hilt like tobacco?

Having looked at how alcohol is marketed to us, I also believe we all need a better understanding of it. Like domestic abuse and mental health issues, alcohol dependence is still exceptionally common yet taboo. Would this change if we were all more aware of it and could talk about it more openly?

Twenty years ago, you would never have admitted to suffering from anxiety or depression on an application form because of the stigma associated with it, but that seems to be changing. I would never have told my employers in the early years of my career that I suffered with anxiety, whereas now, I wouldn't think twice. Perhaps in the future, the stigma around alcohol consumption will change too, and maybe it will be regarded as an illness rather than a character flaw, with employers taking a more sympathetic view of the problem.

As you know, when I started on my journey, I knew very little about alcohol. I wonder whether governments should be doing more to develop our knowledge. Or do they really want us to carry on drinking so that they can continue raising money for the treasury? The reluctance to introduce minimum pricing for alcohol, despite the fact there are many examples of where this has had a positive impact, such as in Scotland, might suggest just that. (13)

I never thought in a million years that I would support such measures, after all, who wants to pay more for their drinks? But if we have evidence that taking such measures prevents people from becoming ill and dying from their drinking, surely governments have a moral duty to do so. That being said, minimum pricing has its critics and I'm sure that the alcohol industry would argue that there are other ways to reduce people's drinking.

We know that alcohol, alongside all the pleasure that it brings, has brought challenges to civilisations and governments throughout time, and some have dabbled with the idea of prohibition being a solution. As we're about to find out, the impact has been varied and whether these attempts have been successful or not depends on how you measure success.

Alcohol Reconsidered

The Alcohol Problem

Sylvain

'It is a capital mistake to theorize before one has data.'

~ Sir Arthur Ignatius Conan Doyle

The aim of this chapter is not to stigmatise alcohol or the people who drink it. Alcohol is a mere beverage, although it has the power to alter the mind of the drinker when consumed in a certain quantity, and it is also highly addictive. Most people can drink regularly without experiencing any problem, but others cannot. Sadly, alcohol-related health issues and deaths are not uncommon in our society.

I have included a range of statistics in this chapter to illustrate how significant some of the harms that alcohol can cause are. Though it may be tempting to skip past this information, I would encourage you not only to read it but to familiarise yourself with it.

It is worth noting that alcohol doesn't just cause problems in developed countries. There is also plenty of evidence to show that alcohol is a public health concern in developing countries too. (1) According to the World Health Organisation, it is the third leading risk factor for poor health globally. (2)

In 2010, the 193 Member States of WHO reached a consensus on a strategy to reduce the harms of alcohol, and it could be argued that the situation is stabilising to a certain extent in developed countries. (3) However, some low-income countries are struggling financially, and for this reason are unable to respond adequately. (4) The budgets allocated to the alcohol problem may vary from one country to another, and simply don't exist in others.

Below are some rather shocking statistics on the alcohol problem in the UK:

- Men accounted for approximately two-thirds of the total number of alcohol-related deaths in 2018. That year, there were 7,551 alcohol-specific deaths in the UK, 5,077 of these deaths (16.4 per 100,000 population) were men, and 2,474 (7.6 per 100,000) were women (5)

- In 2018, it is estimated there were 240 fatal drink-drive accidents (6)

- It is estimated that there were 561,000 violent alcohol-related incidents in 2017/18 (7)

- In England, between 2017 and 2018, there were 357,659 estimated admissions where an alcohol-related disease, injury, or condition was the primary diagnosis or there was an alcohol-related external cause (8)

- A total of 4% of 16 – 24-year-old men drink more than 50 units a week and 3% of women aged 16 – 24 drink more than 35 units a week (9)

- Among adults, 5% of men and 3% of women are estimated to be higher-risk drinkers in England (10)

- For 16 – 24-year-olds, 21% of deaths in males and 9% of deaths in females have been attributed to alcohol consumption (11)

- Around 35% of all Accident & Emergency attendance and ambulance costs may be alcohol-related in England (12)

More statistics on alcohol in the UK can be found on the charity Alcohol Change UK's website https://alcoholchange.org.uk/ or NHS Digital https://digital.nhs.uk/

These facts are not meant to scare you, but to provide hard evidence to show that the alcohol problem is real.

Below are strategies that member states of the World Health Organisation are adopting to address the alcohol problem. They have agreed to:

- Regulate the marketing of alcohol
- Regulate and restructure the availability of alcohol
- Enact appropriate drink-driving policies
- Reduce demand through taxation
- Raise awareness of public health problems relating to alcohol
- Make treatment affordable and accessible
- Implement screening and brief intervention programmes (13)

Information about these strategies and more can be found on The WHO website, https://www.who.int/

While progress in reducing alcohol harm may appear to be slow in some countries, it is encouraging to see that it is at least a topic of consideration.

If your drinking has become a problem, I hope my chapter on support services and treatments will help you to identify what is available and what might be appropriate.

Lesley Miller & Catheryn Kell-Clarke

Is the Answer Prohibition?

Lesley

'Prohibition only drives drunkenness behind closed doors and into dark places, and does not cure it or even diminish it.'

~ Mark Twain

We've looked at some of the significant ills that alcohol can bring to individuals, families, and societies. So, if alcohol is so bad for us, why don't we just ban it completely? We have, after all, made smoking socially unacceptable. Surely the people who claim they can 'take it or leave it' wouldn't mind leaving it if it would eradicate a lot of these problems. Or would this be a bit extreme?

Historically there have been plenty of attempts at banning drinking or at least controlling intake. In fact, during the pandemic, we have seen many countries doing just this.

Prohibition

One of the best-known attempts to tackle the problem of alcohol was the Prohibition which took place in America between 1920 and 1933. Before I started my research for this book, I had always assumed that it had been unsuccessful because after all, America's modern-day issues with the drink are closely matched to our own in the UK. Also, this is what I'd been repeatedly told so I'd always assumed it to be true.

Surprisingly, it wasn't alcohol per se that was thought to be the problem. It was where it was mainly drunk, the saloon, that was deemed to have been the problem. I'm not sure that even I would have fancied the saloon. During this time you were still allowed to consume your own personal stash of alcohol and it could also still be used for religious purposes. You could even get your hands on some 'medicinal whiskey' if you needed it. (1) It was the manufacturing, selling, and importing of alcohol that was prohibited and not a ban on drinking, as I had always imagined.

The saloons posed a range of problems. They were not the cosy kind of establishments like the pub that Cate and Martin were running in the Cotswolds. Instead, they had a reputation of being full of men spending all their wages, getting drunk, and then going home and abusing their wives. (2) It was thought that domestic violence, as it was in other countries, rife at this time. Women, quite understandably, got almightily fed up with this and decided that they'd had enough.

A feminist movement

The idea of prohibition was championed and supported not only by women but by Protestants and progressives too. The Protestants were probably of the opinion that drinking wasn't fitting with their Christian values.

The Women's Christian Temperance Union was actually founded in 1873, long before the Prohibition we are talking about began. They, alongside the Anti-Saloon League, were one of the leading supporters of prohibition. Prohibition it seems, was in part, a feminist movement. In fact, women's lives in America were starting to change throughout this and the next century, as they gained more autonomy and eventually, the right to vote.

The ban officially came into play on 17 January 1920, but interestingly, it might not have been quite as dramatic as we have been led to believe. There had been quite a lot of laws prohibiting alcohol in one way or another over the previous fifty years. During the First World War, the distillation of spirits was banned to preserve grain supplies. There was of course great sadness for those who loved the saloon, and some even held actual 'funerals' for them. (3) Back then people were divided into two groups; the 'Wets', who were opposed to prohibition, and the 'Drys', who wanted alcohol banned. I'm sure a lot of us can relate to the 'Wets' when many of our own pubs have been closed throughout the pandemic.

Criminal gangs

Of course, what happened next is what always happens when you make a drug illegal; alcohol went underground. Criminals saw this as an excellent business opportunity. They began smuggling spirits and started making liquor from the alcohol used in the industry by mixing it with chemicals. Illegal distillation got underway, and if you were that way inclined, you could get your hands on some moonshine liquor or some 'bathtub gin'. These were reported to have tasted revolting, and they could have killed you too. (4) No doubt I would have been up for trying them. You might have been doing this drinking at a 'speakeasy' which is the name for a place that you could get an illicit drink. The difference between a saloon and a speakeasy is that women could go to the latter.

This carried on for a good number of years, but then there was the Wall Street Crash in 1929, the most devastating stock market crash America had ever seen. This in turn led to the Great Depression that lasted until the late thirties.

Essentially, Prohibition ended because people needed jobs, and the country needed the money from the taxation of alcohol that was currently going to organised gangs. What this attempt at prohibition had done was to virtually wipe out an entire industry. In more recent examples of prohibition, we can see the devastating impact that it has had on those who work within the hospitality trade.

Success or failure?

It's easy to say that prohibition didn't work, as this is what the history books tell us. There is no doubt that it must have been nothing short of a nightmare to police, and there was clearly no collective agreement that the nation wanted to stop drinking. However, eventually, levels of drinking did return to pre-Prohibition levels so if you're judging the amount people drank over the long-term, you could say it failed.

It is, however, worth pointing out that during this time alcohol consumption did decrease overall and the impact of this was that there were fewer hospital admissions, fewer drunken arrests, and fewer cases of liver cirrhosis. (5) The traditional saloons became a thing of the past. So, if you look at it like that, it was actually a big success.

As Cate discovered, when she was researching her chapter on the marketing of alcohol, its legacy was far-reaching, and the advertising of liquor and spirits was banned on American television networks for most of the twentieth century.

America may boast the best-known example of prohibition, but there have been several attempts at solving the problems that drinking brings across the world. Some have been much more successful than you might have been led to believe, with perhaps a few exceptions. Is it a permanent solution though?

Australia and New Zealand

America's attempts were certainly more successful than Australia and New Zealand's. Their attempts at moderating drinking lasted half a century. Both countries brought in prohibition during the Second World War, and it was referred to as 'The Six O'Clock Swill'. It was introduced as part of an austerity measure and it was also aimed at improving public morality. These countries faced the same problems as America, including that of domestic violence. It was brought into law in 1919 after pressure from the Temperance Movement and thus, the pubs had to close their doors at 6 pm.

So, men finished work at 5 pm and the pubs shut at 6 pm. Can you guess what happened next? Yes. As you can imagine, a culture of heavy, fast drinking developed very quickly. Following a day's work, men would go to the pub and drink as quickly as they possibly could in the one hour that they had to do it. The new law had been intended to curb drunkenness and crime. However, sending men home early to their families actually had the opposite effect. There were more car crashes between 6 pm and 8 pm as drunken men would drive home as there were very few, if any, drink driving laws. There were also more reports of assaults on women and children during these hours, and it would be common for men to purchase more alcohol to consume at home. You couldn't then, in all honesty, call it a resounding success. (6)

Russia

Let's take a look at Russia. The Russians have a reputation for being very hearty drinkers. Perhaps the reason for this because of how socially acceptable it has been in the country historically.

It is reported that back in 1860, the sale of alcohol, namely vodka, was where the government received 40 per cent of its revenue (7) and throughout the twentieth century there were various unpopular attempts at prohibition. Mikhail Gorbachev attempted to address the issue with restrictions on buying alcohol and penalties for public drunkenness, but ultimately, they didn't work.

This might not come as a surprise when you consider that it was only in 2011 that beer was even considered to be alcoholic. Prior to that, anything less than 10 per cent proof was considered a foodstuff. (8)

Russia has also experienced the societal ills that are linked to alcohol, such as violent crime and domestic violence. What the authorities have done, however, is to spend time addressing this problem. Over time, they have increased the price of alcohol alongside minimum pricing. In addition to this, they have also banned the sale of alcohol after 11 pm and have given their advertising laws a lot of attention. It is illegal to drink on the streets and if you do, you can expect to be fined.

The impact of this is that ultimately, Russians are drinking less and living longer. It's thought that between 2003 and 2018 alcohol consumption reduced by a staggering 43 per cent. According to a World Health Organisation report, life expectancy in Russia hit a record in 2018 with men's now reaching an average of 68, and women 78. (9)

Scotland

Scotland is another country that is attempting to address some of the health issues caused by heavy drinking. On 1 May 2018, the Scottish government introduced minimum pricing for alcohol meaning that a unit could not be sold for less than 50p. The idea in Scotland was to target those who are experiencing the most harm from alcohol while not affecting moderate drinkers. It is a little premature to say what the long-term impact of this will be, but early indications show that alcohol consumption did decrease during the first year.

South Africa

More recent attempts at prohibition come from countries who have used this as a way of tackling some of the problems brought about by Covid-19.

For example, South Africa banned the transportation of both alcohol and cigarettes for five months during the pandemic. The aim of this was to keep people healthy so that they would be less likely to become seriously ill with the virus, and to ease pressure on the health system. Prior to Covid-19 it is thought that around 30 per cent of all hospital admissions in South Africa were alcohol related. (10)

As we know, some of the negative consequences of prohibition are an increase in the illegal sale of alcohol on the black market. Mirroring what happened in America, reports suggest that this is exactly what happened. It isn't easy to find accurate data on this, but one can assume this would have led to a number of deaths through poisoning and overdoses. There are also wider implications for the people who work in the industry. A significant number of people lost their jobs, and this led to a lack of revenue from alcohol sales for the treasury.

That being said, the benefits of this ban were simply staggering. There was a significant reduction in nearly all types of crime including murder, rape, robbery, and domestic violence to name but a few. In addition to that, it is thought that hospital trauma admissions were down by around 66.9 per cent. The upshot of this is that while many other countries saw an increase in excess deaths because of the pandemic, South Africa actually saw fewer excess deaths than normal. (11)

This, however, was a temporary ban, and you might argue that if it had been more permanent, there might have been less compliance and greater public outrage. I don't think prohibition has ever gone down too well with the public in any country in the long term, whatever the benefits to public health.

Should governments be doing more?

The question remains then if we know that alcohol consumption is a public health issue for many countries across the world, and it is, what are we going to do about it? I think the first thing we can conclude is that dealing with this problem needs to be more of a priority. I personally am not convinced that some countries are taking the problem seriously as they should. We can also look at some of the policies and strategies that governments have adopted that appear to have worked.

Here in the UK, we don't even have laws on the labelling of alcohol with adequate health warnings. Worryingly, many products still contain old health guidelines. According to a research conducted by the Alcoholic Health Alliance, 70 per cent of containers across the UK are still missing the correct information. (12) If you've got a bottle or a can of something alcoholic in front of you now, take look at the label. Does it give you, as a consumer, adequate health information?

As mentioned earlier, our government does *know* that alcohol is a big problem. I'll leave the question as to whether they are doing enough to address it for you to decide.

A money spinner

We know that one of the negative consequences of prohibition is the loss of revenue for the industry and the treasury, but does it have to be so? Pubs are places where we enjoy gathering with family and friends and given some of the restrictions we have seen during the pandemic, it is clear to see their value. It would be devastating to lose all our pubs and bars. Maybe now is the time for them to start offering a wider selection of alcohol-free drinks. Perhaps they will have to if the trend of younger generations turning their back on alcohol continues.

Education

One thing that is clear is that we need a better understanding of alcohol, of the benefits that it brings, and of the problems that it can create. If we are to make informed choices about our health, we need to know more about what alcohol is and how it works. I'm sure a lot of this information is taught in schools, but to what extent? What happens after people leave school? Should business leaders and employers be playing a key role in making sure everyone is properly informed? Given how many days a year are lost to sick days and a lack of productivity, it may be in their best interests to do so.

I am of the belief that alcohol should be much higher up on many governments' agenda, and that they should be thinking about the long-term implications of alcohol consumption, not just the immediate money-making opportunities. You don't need to be a genius to see that dangerous alcohol consumption and its implications must be costing us more than it is bringing in. And yet, although Public Health England hopes to create a smoke-free society by 2030, there is no mention of alcohol in its health priorities for the next five years. (13)

Not all of you will be UK based. How clear are you about what is happening in your own country? I know we all like to think that we are terribly advanced, but why is more not being done? There must be a way that we can reduce the harms of alcohol without ruining the entire industry. There is plenty to consider here, and the more I think about it, the more shocking it is that alcohol isn't much higher up on the public health agenda.

As we emerge from the Covid-19 pandemic we are in quite a unique position, as the focus of many governments is public health. While prohibition is probably undesirable, there should be more attempts made to ensure that the public is given more substantial information to make informed choices. The key of course will be achieving this without destroying an industry that is, in our opinion at least, to be greatly valued.

Support Services and Treatments

Sylvain

'The only mistake you can make, is not asking for help.'

~ Sandeep Jauhar

As you know by now, we believe that moderation is a good route to consider if abstinence is too big a goal to set. However, it is worth noting that controlled drinking is difficult to achieve. It is also worth knowing that treatment services exist. Those who cannot achieve moderation or controlled drinking on their own may need professional support.

This chapter is intended to give you a list of the provision of alcohol support services in Britain. The UK follows a 4-tier model, which is important to understand for people to identify and access the right treatment for them. Here is an outline of how the tiered approach to alcohol services works.

The onus is very much on the individual asking for help rather than it being offered, but people don't generally seem to understand how to get the help they need.

Tier 1

Tier 1 services are not specific alcohol treatment services, but any public or private sector service which are points of the first contact for individuals. Examples are doctor's surgeries, job centres, housing or social services. They are also provided in general healthcare, social care, education, or criminal justice settings.

This type of intervention would be appropriate for anyone who needs information, advice, signposting or referral to specialist alcohol treatment services.

At this level, alcohol related information and advice are provided by the workers of these services. They are also responsible for screening and referrals to specialised alcohol treatments.

To access this kind of support people can self-refer or just present themselves to these services.

Tier 2

Tier 2 treatment would be appropriate for people who have an alcohol problem and want support to address it. It is for individuals who are concerned about their own drinking, or that of a loved one, and wish to engage in alcohol treatment to address such concerns.

Interventions include the provision of alcohol-related information, advice for individuals and triage assessment. This is an initial assessment to gather some information about the individual and their drinking. It allows the workers to establish a threshold of needs for the individuals to be evaluated.

After this first step, a brief intervention plan is devised for the individual if their problem does not require a structured treatment. If they are presenting complex needs, they may require a more robust treatment plan. A comprehensive assessment of the individual is carried out to allow the Tier 2 service to have a holistic understanding of the individual's situation.

At this point, a more comprehensive treatment plan is put forward for the individual, which may include attending group work sessions, one to one counselling sessions and any other psychosocial interventions, as appropriate. Mutual aid groups and peer support activities as well as a referral to Tier 3 services can be done in the Tier 2 service.

Psychosocial interventions usually include talking therapies, counselling, one to one or group work sessions. Such interventions can include psychotherapy with social activities, like group meetings and art works.

Tier 2 interventions may be delivered separately from Tier 3 but will often also be available in the same setting and by the same staff. To access this kind of support people can self-refer, or be referred by a professional, family member or friend.

Tier 3

Tier 3 treatment would be appropriate for people who have completed Tier 2. They will have achieved a level of recovery by not drinking or will have significantly reduced their consumption. Tier 3 interventions include the provision of community-based specialised alcohol assessment, co-ordinated care planned treatment and alcohol specialist liaison.

Tier 3 interventions are normally delivered in specialised alcohol treatment services with their own premises in the community, or hospital sites. They might also be delivered through outreach work, such as travelling from place to place for short periods of time in generic healthcare services or other agencies. Alternatively, they can be delivered as domiciliary care or home visits to individuals whose movements are restricted.

To access this kind of support, individuals may need to have previously engaged at Tier 2 level, and Tier 3 will be a continuation of their care.

Tier 4

Tier 4 treatment would be appropriate for people who have completed both Tier 2 and Tier 3 treatments.

At this level, treatment may involve specialist residentials which are planned and coordinated to ensure continuity of care and aftercare.

Ideal settings for providing inpatient alcohol treatment are specialised and dedicated inpatient or residential substance misuse units or wards.

Taking charge

As a practitioner, I have worked across all tiers, but mainly in Tier 2 and 3 services. I have supported individuals and families, facilitated group work sessions, and carried out one-to-one sessions. I have experience in performing alcohol detoxification activities, helping with funding processes for patients, and organising rehab for clients.

It is difficult to witness how people's lives go wrong because of alcohol. I have often felt so sad and powerless. It is challenging seeing people trapped in such a cycle of alcohol addiction and watching them continue to drink at great risk to their physical and mental health. Sometimes I have longed for a magic wand to try and wave the addiction away, but it's simply not that easy. Sometimes you just know where someone's drinking is going to take them, and you feel powerless to do anything about it.

On the flip side, it is rewarding to see positive changes happen. A client might have come to you with a very poor prognosis, and it is wonderful to watch them turn their lives around. It is rewarding to be able to empower people in such a life-changing, and often a life-saving way.

In my 16 years of supporting individuals with alcohol problems, I have experienced the good, the bad, and the ugly of alcohol. I have seen people recover, I have also seen people relapse, and I have seen people die. As I already mentioned, alcohol addiction is not a death sentence because many people do recover. The way forward is to admit that there is a problem, and then to find the right help. Treatment for alcohol issues are not compulsory. Therefore, the responsibility lies with patients to decide what they want to do about their drinking. But there is definitely hope.

One thing that may be helpful is to be open to change and seek help to make that change. My advice is to seek professional help and not to try and do it alone. Recovery by oneself does not work in most cases. Also, research has shown that shame, guilt, stigma, and denial are all-powerful barriers to seeking treatment. (1, 2)

A steady reduction

Alcohol professionals are the best people to approach when drinking is no longer fun. The rule of thumb is to try and reduce your drinking by 10 per cent each week. However, people usually find it difficult to follow these rules. For example, if someone was drinking 10 cans of lager a day, they can start their reduction by drinking nine cans per day for a week, then eight cans per day for another week and so on until they reach the tenth week with just one can remaining. This may only work for someone who has not developed the disease of alcoholism. (3)

Sometimes it might be helpful for people in recovery to work with a life coach or a mentor who can support them in maintaining the changes that they need to make. For some people, attending an Alcoholic Anonymous (AA) meeting and following the 12 Steps, are a crucial key to recovery from alcoholism. Nevertheless, this is not to say that people cannot recover by managing their drinking.

Unfortunately, I do have memories of those who did not make it. Some of my patients have died a sudden death due to an illness such as bleeding of the oesophagus, liver disease or pancreatitis. When people are aware of a health concern, this does not usually deter them from drinking. Clients usually say that something has got to click in their mind first, or they have got to reach 'rock bottom' before they can start to engage in meaningful change.

All the above makes the steady reduction more difficult to achieve, and alcohol related illnesses start to set in or continue to progress such as the Wernicke-Korsakoff's Syndrome or WKS.

Wernicke-Korsakoff's Syndrome

I used to have clients in local hostels, sometimes over 50 male residents. In these hostels, it was not uncommon to come across people with Wernicke-Korsakoff's syndrome. This is a condition commonly referred to as 'wet brain' or 'beriberi', where someone will act as if they are drunk, even if they have not had a drink. WKS is a combination of two conditions occurring at the same time; Wernicke's encephalopathy and Korsakoff's psychosis. These are caused by brain damage due to the lack of vitamin B1.

Some symptoms can include confabulation and disorientation. Confabulation is a symptom of various memory disorders in which made-up stories fill in any gaps in memory. The term confabulation was used for the first time in 1900 by a German psychiatrist called Karl Bonhoeffer. He described confabulation as being:

'...when a person gives false answers or answers that sound fantastical or made up.' (4)

This condition is usually missed and not diagnosed by doctors, which makes its morbidity rate high. High doses of thiamine and strong vitamin B compounds are usually prescribed by doctors to help or prevent WKS. The good news is that **people do recover** from alcohol addiction.

Recovering from alcohol addiction or alcoholism

Recovery is a journey that starts by accepting that there is a problem. It is difficult for anyone to make any change when they are in denial. People usually do not want to admit the problem, because alcohol is their comforter or their hiding place. It is difficult for such individuals to put away the thing that gives them meaning or helps them to cope with life.

Admitting the problem is the first step to understanding what treatment or recovery means, how important treatment is, and what it requires. Sometimes people engage in treatment to please others, or to escape the nagging of a partner or family member when they are not ready. It is hard to make any progress if a client isn't self-motivated.

Some people deliberately refuse to accept or acknowledge that they have a problem, and loved ones need to understand that denial is all part of the addiction. Others simply don't realise there is help out there. Some are aware it is there, but simply don't want to engage in the recovery process. Some have had a certain amount of success with treatment in the past, and then, for whatever reason, choose not to continue. Perhaps not enough is done to promote the help that is there. Perhaps more needs to be done to raise people's awareness of the services available, or to minimise their apprehensions, fears, mistrust, or frustrations.

Recovery may follow the 'Cycle of Change'. This cycle was proposed in a 1982 paper by American academics, James Prochaska, and Carlo C. DiClemente. (5, 6)

Prochaska and DiClemente explain how people can be in complete denial of their problems. After some time, they can start thinking about it, act, and in the end, sustain their actions. Or they may fall back into unhealthy behaviour again. They called it the 'Cycle of Change' which comprises the stages of pre-contemplation, contemplation, decision, action, exit or relapse. An awareness of this cycle is useful for professionals, so they can use the correct intervention at the right time. For instance, motivational interviewing may be appropriate to support people in contemplation and relapse prevention for people in the maintenance stage. This may vary according to individuals.

This book aims to give readers the information they may need to make their own choices. If individuals are not physically dependent on alcohol to function, and they do not have withdrawal symptoms, then they can decide to reduce their drinking and stop as they wish. However, if they experience severe withdrawal symptoms in the absence of alcohol, they may need professional assistance to stop drinking and this may involve engaging in the 4-Tier model.

If recovery is to be achieved one way or the other, it is important to also include a positive environment and a helpful and supportive social network in the recovery plan. It is the effort of all parties; the individuals, significant others, and the professionals that contribute to meaningful and sustainable recovery from alcohol addiction. These treatments are carried out confidentially. The choice is theirs to involve a third person in their recovery journey or not.

Case Studies

Sylvain

'I am very serious about no alcohol, no drugs. Life is too beautiful.'

~ Jim Carrey

Throughout my career, I have seen people turn their lives around after being caught in the cycle of alcohol addiction for years. The case studies presented here are a few examples of people who have recovered from alcohol addiction, and those who did not. I don't expect that you are drinking at this level, but I have included them to raise your awareness and for your interest.

There is a myth that 'once an addict, always an addict'. Some significant numbers of people do recover from alcohol addiction. That being said, if you have ever been addicted to alcohol, you should remain vigilant and self-aware, even after 25 years of abstinence. There is scientific evidence to show that once people have recovered from alcohol addiction, they are prone to relapse at any time if they start to drink again. (1)

If abstinence is the best choice for you, then you must avoid drinking at all costs. But as we have already stressed in this book, it is not realistic or desirable for everyone.

Mr AA

Mr AA first attended my alcohol awareness group in 2011 and declared that he was not really a drinker, or an alcoholic, or alcohol dependent. He used to boast about the fact that he was educated, had a good job, and made a lot of money. He was very proud of the fact that he had bought a good house in an expensive part of London. He used to compare himself with some members of the group who were living in hostels and sneaking cans of beer in their jackets as they attended the group. As the group facilitator, I had to explain that alcohol does not discriminate. It affects people's lives in the same way, regardless of their social status or whether you are rich or poor. Some group members were not impressed with the bragging and challenged him, but others were not bothered. They could clearly see that he was not really any different from them, even if he was wearing fancier and cleaner clothes.

During one session another participant asked him, 'So why are you here if you think that you don't have an alcohol problem?' Perhaps I should point out here that your doctor, your family members, the police or the court can't coerce you into treatment if you haven't acknowledged that you have a problem.

Mr AA knew there was some problem to a certain extent, but he was in denial and the other group members could see that. He told his story saying that he was a successful salesman who frequently met customers in fancy restaurants and discussed business over a pint of beer or a glass of wine. He would also have a glass or two of wine at home with dinner. He informed us that he had no worries until he had an accident, and his blood test showed some issues with his liver. He was formally diagnosed with an alcohol problem and sent to the local treatment service and that was how he came to the alcohol awareness group.

He was not honest with us or himself about his drinking. He was in denial, and he was trying to minimise his struggle by presenting himself as a superman. He used to say in the rounds of introductions to group members that he had been shot twice, stabbed three times and he had fallen 30 feet off a cliff, and hadn't been killed. This, he had decided, was evidence that he was invincible, and that alcohol could not kill him. He stated that he was surprised and shocked with his diagnosis because he had always considered his drinking to be social. Thus, his response was *'How can a social drinker have developed a liver problem?'* He did not know that he was drinking more than eight units of alcohol every day, which is well above the UK Chief Medical Officer's 'safest' drinking recommendations. He said that he was shocked, but he kept on minimising the warnings and continued to drink despite attending the day programme and learning tips and facts about alcohol. His wife was more concerned about his health than he was, as she used to drop him for the group sessions and come back later to pick him up. However, there were times when he used to leave the day programme early before his wife came to pick him up. She used to call the reception when she could not find him. She would later discover that he was sitting in a pub or had gone to the park to drink.

Mr AA completed many detoxes, but also relapsed many times before he was finally admitted to a hospice for terminal liver cancer. He continued to drink, saying that he needed to enjoy his remaining moments on Earth. He died in 2019 in his early 60s.

Mr BB

Mr BB was drinking a 70cl bottle of vodka every day despite being aware of his decompensated liver. He was continually in and out of the hospital and finally admitted to A & E after being found intoxicated and unconscious in the street. Prior to that, he had been found on three different occasions, drinking hand sanitiser in the toilet. He was subsequently transferred to a mental health unit while his treatment for alcohol use disorder continued. He had more than 15 detoxes and rehabilitation treatments which accounted for approximately £300,000 of public funds. I mention this to emphasise the scale of the alcohol problem in the UK, and to highlight his struggle. I think it shows how hard he had tried to recover. I would like to make the point that public funds are available for people who want to reconsider their alcohol use. His story could have been different, possibly even worse, if there were no public funds in place.

Mr BB also had diabetes and he was in danger of losing his leg, but this did not stop him from drinking. When he managed to attend an appointment, he was tearful and emotional, feeling powerless over his drinking. I recall him crying on one occasion saying that he did not want to die. However, once he left the service, the first thing that he would do was to have a drink. It was desperately sad to witness his struggle and see his dilemma. I have lost contact with Mr BB since I worked with him, and sadly, I don't know how his struggle played out.

Ms CC

Ms CC attended a structured day programme in 2015. She was drinking alcohol and using cocaine. She was in an abusive relationship and she had five children. Three of her children were in foster care and two living with her mother. She was living in a two-bedroom flat on a council estate where her friends supplied her with drink and drugs.

There were marks of physical abuse on her body at times, but she had the tendency of normalising the violence that was perpetrated towards her. On one occasion, she disclosed in a group work session that her partner slapped her face with a TV remote control, and she seemed to think that this was okay. The other group members did not agree, and the group discussion helped to open her mind. The following week she walked out of this relationship, but she did not attend the day programme for two weeks. When she returned, she said in the group session, *'I want to change, but the idiot in me wants to remain the same.'* That is called ambivalence: a state of mind where individuals have a conversation with themselves, and where they are usually torn between two forces. One positive force which drives them upward and one negative force which pulls them downward. Usually, the latter is stronger. At the end of the day, such a person needs a push upward to make the change that they desire.

Ms CC was in the right place at the right time, and she took the opportunity that was offered to engage in meaningful and long-lasting recovery. On that day, she made the decision to go into residential treatment.

Ms CC regularly attended the day programme and completed all the necessary tasks. She also engaged in all other aspects of her care plan, and she was awarded funding for detoxification and residential rehabilitation. She subsequently completed the rehabilitation programme and the aftercare programme. Ms CC is now completely abstinent. She completed detox and rehab in 2015. She did have a relapse after two years and subsequently drank now and again for the following year. Eventually, she decided to stop for good. Ms CC has not had a drink since 2018, and she is now married and has a beautiful two-year-old girl. She has started her own business and she is working from home and raising her children. She says that she is enjoying life with her family and she has definitely moved on from drugs and alcohol.

Mr DD

Mr DD was a British male originally from Bangladesh. He was a trained chef who developed a drinking habit and subsequently lost his job and his self-confidence. He became homeless as he separated from his wife. She had custody of their children. Because of the repeated domestic violence episodes, there was an injunction against him, and he was not allowed to visit his family. There is empirical evidence of partner violence amongst people who misuse alcohol. Let us remember that alcohol is a depressant drug that makes people do things that they don't remember or they later regret. It also exacerbates anger and triggers impulsive behaviour. This is why drinkers are not fond of being challenged or nagged by their partners, as this can result in episodes of domestic violence.

Mr DD felt depressed and hopeless and was referred to our service. He was residing at a local hostel for over 50s and he was drinking between 18 and 24 cans of Stella Artois every day. He was tearful and emotional whenever he attended the group work sessions.

It took a lot of effort to convince Mr DD that he could recover from alcohol addiction. When someone has lost self-confidence and hope, they are usually subject to negative automatic thoughts and their way of thinking changes: they catastrophise, they feel hopeless most of the time, they become anxious and depressed. When individuals are in such a dark place, they do not believe in the light at the end of the tunnel and Mr DD did not see any light at the end of his. Nevertheless, things got better in the end, and he was empowered enough to embark on the recovery journey.

Despite losing his hope and confidence, Mr DD was attending the support group regularly, and he started to show the motivation to change. With the support he received from the treatment service, he was afforded funding and went to residential treatment where he completed the programme after six months. He subsequently came back to London and he was reunited with his family. He has since resumed his career as a head chef. I have had no further contact with Mr DD.

Miss EE

Ms EE presented to our service in 2019 as a chaotic, drinking single mum with two young children, then aged four and five. She was referred by social services after allegedly smacking her daughter at the school gate. The report said that Miss EE had smelled of alcohol when the incident occurred. There were also social services and police reports of domestic violence between Ms EE and her ex-partner, the children's father. Ms EE was not willing to engage, claiming that she had experienced a bad past experience with support services. She attended two meetings whilst completely intoxicated, and at others was unable to participate meaningfully, to the point where they had to be adjourned.

After several key work sessions, which included motivational interviewing and harm reduction sessions, Miss EE started to engage and began to reduce her alcohol intake. She developed more insights into the impact of her drinking on her mental and physical health, but mostly on her children.

In time Miss EE became even more motivated and began reviewing her social network. She took the opportunity of the 2020 lockdown to unfriend some unhelpful people in her life, and she focused more on her children, her mother, her job, and her recovery. She produced monthly blood tests which showed a reduction and cessation of alcohol use. Miss EE is now a social drinker, and she plans with the social services when she wants to attend an event where alcohol is likely to be present, and she has learnt how to drink moderately and stop when she needs to stop.

I think these stories are proof of just how big and how indiscriminate the problem of alcohol abuse is. Although some people recover, sadly, others do not. (2)

Our relationships with alcohol can be complex, and like any other relationship, there are good and bad times involved. As we've seen, problem drinking has led to a ban on alcohol in the past, but it seems that for social and economic reasons, society cannot or won't do without it. Whether we like it or not, alcohol is here to stay.

As we have seen in previous chapters, if it was banned, people would go underground, because alcohol is also part of peoples' social lives in many countries. This means that people will still make alcohol and drink it even if governments try to impose bans or prohibitions.

To get things into perspective, it is important to remember that many people drink, and relatively few develop a problem with alcohol. However, it is encouraging to know that as a practitioner, I am helping to save lives by supporting people in making meaningful changes.

Conclusion

Cate

'You can't go back and change the beginning, but you can start where you are and change the ending.'

~ C.S. Lewis

Hopefully, by reading our book you have learnt something about yourself and your relationship with alcohol. Perhaps you were intrigued by the Gin Epidemic, or maybe you were shocked by how much money is spent on advertising alcohol when we are essentially prepared to buy it anyway. Perhaps all those frightening facts about what alcohol does to your mind and your body have helped you to reconsider your relationship with drink. Maybe you related to my tale about being shy and using alcohol as a crutch or Lesley's tales of deep despair and guilt. Whatever it was that spoke directly to you, you can now move forward and begin to reconsider your relationship with alcohol.

The quote by C.S. Lewis at the start of this chapter resonates so much with me. None of us can change the past, but when we look back, perhaps we can find something, maybe just one thing that we can feel positive about. Writing this book has given me the chance to think deeply about my drinking and how it was affecting not just me, but the others around me as well as my health. I've learned to slow down and not try to be the 'super woman' who needed the reward of a glass or two when I had completed my often ridiculously long to-do list. The pandemic and 2020 allowed me the opportunity to turn things around, to slow down, and to really reflect on my life choices. Again, that all sounds pretty corny, but corny or not, that's what happened.

For me, it's the realisation that I don't need to have a drink to be liked and to have a good time. Saying that, however, while I don't think

I'll ever give up drinking completely, I do know that I can consciously consider my drinking options now. My husband, wallet, and body all thank me for that.

As a teacher, I know all too well that learning is a life-long process. I never want to stop exploring things that interest me and, alcohol, in whatever form it may take, certainly does. Whether or not I choose to pour it down my throat and actually drink the stuff is up to me just as what you decide to take away from reading this book is, in the end, up to you. Maybe you will now decide that you want to dig deeper into understanding alcohol, maybe you now know you definitely want to cut back. Perhaps you will recommend this book to a friend. Our goal, whatever you decide to do, is that you, at the very least, will reconsider your options and that this book might just be the catalyst you need to make any changes.

2020 will be a year we will all be talking about for a very long time, and yet for so many people, it was a year that brought some positives. While it stank on a number of levels, it was also the year that I finally decided that I did in fact like myself. Whether it was being able to think more clearly because I wasn't drinking so much, I'm not sure, or maybe it was the hour or so I allowed myself each morning to just walk. Who can say? I really don't know. I do know, however, that without Covid-19, I would be rushing around, trying to do a million things at once, and without a doubt, still teaching.

Whatever it was, something clicked and thank goodness it did. Do I regret the fact that the 'click' didn't happen sooner? Perhaps, for example, when my old mum was still alive, she would have been very proud of the 'new' me. But like I said before, regrets are a complete waste of time. The first step starts as soon as you are ready to take it.

It may not have to be such a catastrophic 'perfect storm' of bad things to make you start to change your alcohol options, but whatever it takes, remember there is always someone who has been in your position and there are many organisations that can help you.

Stay safe everyone. Look after yourself and each other. Be kind. Tomorrow is another day, and it could be the start of something big for you.

Best Wishes

Cate

Lesley Miller & Catheryn Kell-Clarke

Lesley

'Many things which cannot be overcome when they are together yield themselves up when taken little by little.'

~ Plutarch

Alcohol has been around since before we were even here, and for reasons that we've discussed, it isn't likely to vanish at any point in the future. It's down to us then to ensure that we are as knowledgeable as we can be so that if we decide to continue to drink, we can enjoy the benefits without damaging our mental and physical health.

When we initially discussed our vision for *Alcohol Reconsidered*, we had a number of aims in mind. We wanted to ensure that anyone reading this who is a bit perplexed about why they drink understands a bit more and stops feeling guilty. Yes, we need to be responsible for our actions, but persecuting ourselves doesn't help us drink less. We were keen for readers to be aware that any safe reduction in drinking will likely lead to better physical and mental health, and to consider that complete abstinence isn't the only solution. I hope that we have provided you with enough information to explore some of the issues surrounding alcohol in a way that doesn't either over-simplify or over-complicate the matter.

As Cate said, I'm sure none of us will forget 2020 in a hurry. Obviously, the pandemic affected our lives in different ways, and I'm sure that many of us used alcohol to cope with the challenges and difficulties it presented. I wonder how many people will have developed a more complex relationship with alcohol as a result? I am sure that there will be some interesting statistics to analyse further down the line.

Alongside the problems, the pandemic provided me with an opportunity to reflect on life and to co-write this book. I'm almost certain that this wouldn't have happened if Cate hadn't come on board, because I would have either lacked the confidence, or I would have kept putting it off. I can't thank her enough for her positivity, kindness and for not judging me when I've told her some of the things that I am most embarrassed about. It still seems a bit bizarre that we haven't seen each other in person in nearly two years, and that all of this has been conducted through the wonders of modern technology.

It has been such an interesting process, and at times it has been very challenging. It's been hard putting into words the problems my drinking has caused, but at the same time, it's been liberating getting it all down on paper. Keeping a log of your thoughts can lead to all sorts of interesting discoveries, and I would really recommend this as a strategy for untangling some of your own thoughts and beliefs. Who knows, you might even write a book of your own?

As I said, I'm not a completely reformed character and I do still drink, so my relationship with alcohol will remain under the microscope for now. I'll continue to ponder the negative aspects that drinking brings us while enjoying the social aspects.

In the UK, the pubs have been closed for much of the last year and this has really brought into sharp focus their value and the role that they play in society. I hope at some point to be able to celebrate with Cate. Perhaps we will even meet Sylvain in 'real-life' so that we can thank him for sharing his experience and expertise with us over a glass of wine.

The next steps for Cate and me are to develop our online course, and I know that we are both itching to start writing our next book. We really believe that we should all know more about alcohol and we will strive to help as many people as we can to understand more. Once a teacher, always a teacher. We will continue to analyse our own relationships with alcohol, and we will keep on talking about it with our friends.

The discussions I have had with mine have been genuinely fascinating, and it's interesting that the more I opened up to them, the more they told me about their own experiences. I was genuinely surprised by how much my friends confessed to drinking. We often just assume that we have a fair idea about who the big drinkers and moderate drinkers are. As we've discussed, it can be a very hidden problem.

One of the most important things I learned on this journey is just how common drinking too much is. I am hopeful that by talking about the issues more freely, we can play our part in breaking down the stigma associated with alcohol and big drinkers.

We hope that you've enjoyed our book and wish you all the very best with your own journey. If you would like to find out more about our courses or want to read our blog, you can find information on our website, www.alcoholreconsidered.com.

Finally, we really want to help as many people as we can. If you have time to write us a quick, honest review on Amazon, we would be most grateful.

And with that, I'm going to pour myself a guilt-free glass of ice-cold champagne.

Cheers!

Acknowledgements

This book would not have been possible to write without the help and support of our family and friends. We are most grateful to everybody who has shared their stories, offered us advice and support, and given us feedback on what we have written.

In particular, we would like to thank the following people: Sylvain Tiecoura, Christina Teles, Tola Akanmu, Martin Clarke, Jayac Heal, Annette Miller, Leanne Harman, Kate Frazer, Lucy Spaull, Sally Spaull, Donna Rutherford, Jenny Barnett, Sarah Boldero, Alison Underwood, Linda Austin, Sharon Bristow, Debbie Eaton, Lynne McCormack, Paul Somerville, Marion Veness, Oliver Grantham, Lindsey Velcic, Louise Summers, Steve Curtis, Jo Reilly, Auntie Irene, Katarzyna Kujava, Susan Kissoon, Caroline Curtis, Shig Hayre, Ken Scott and Graham Relton.

All of you have given so generously of your time and expertise. We are indebted to you all and promise to buy the first drink when we see you.

We would also like to thank our cover designer Madeline Chapman and our editor, Lucy Benyon. This is our first book, so they've needed bucket loads of patience. Madeline has had to design about 200 versions of the front cover and blurb and even as ex-teachers, we couldn't have tackled the content and commas without Lucy.

Finally, we would like to thank Professor David Nutt for granting us permission to cite his work as readily as we wished. If you are looking for another book about alcohol, we strongly recommend that you read his book, 'Drink? The New Science of Alcohol and Your Health'.

Thank you.

References

What is Alcohol?
1. https://dictionary.cambridge.org/dictionary/english/drug
2. https://brewminate.com/drinking-in-victorian-and-edwardian-britain/
3. Nutt, David. *Drink? The New Science of Alcohol & Your Health.* London: Hodder & Stoughton Ltd, 2020
4. https://www.talktofrank.com/drugs-a-z
5. https://www.ucsf.edu/news/2012/01/98513/study-offers-clue-why-alcohol-addicting
6. https://alcoholchange.org.uk/alcohol-facts/fact-sheets/is-alcohol-addictive
7. https://www.sciencedaily.com/releases/2010/10/101018112308.htm
8. ibid
9. https://www.healthline.com/health-news/lateral-habenula-responsible-for-alcholism-040814#Genetics-and-Social-Factors-Play-a-Role

A Very Brief History of Alcohol
1. https://news.berkeley.edu/2014/07/01/drunken-monkeys-and-our-thirst-for-booze/
2. https://theconversation.com/why-young-people-are-drinking-less-and-what-older-drinkers-can-learn-from-them-133020
3. https://www.sciencemag.org/news/2012/03/sexually-rejected-flies-turn-booze
4. Forsyth, Mark. *A Short History of Drunkenness.* London: Penguin Random House, 2017

5. https://www.realmofhistory.com/2018/07/06/barley-beer-late-bronze-age-mesopotamia
6. Forsyth, Mark. *A Short History of Drunkenness.* London: Penguin Random House, 2017
7. http://dictionnaire.sensagent.leparisien.fr/History_of_alcoholic_beverages/en-en/
8. https://www.ancient.eu/article/1033/beer-in-ancient-egypt/
9. Forsyth, Mark. *A Short History of Drunkenness.* London: Penguin Random House, 2017
10. https://www.dailymail.co.uk/home/books/article-2118886/Binge-drinking-equal-rights-Ancient-Egypt-WOMEN-IN-ANCIENT-EGYPT-BY-BARBARA-WATTERSON.html
11. Forsyth, Mark. *A Short History of Drunkenness.* London: Penguin Random House, 2017
12. http://www.users.globalnet.co.uk/~loxias/symposium.htm
13. Forsyth, Mark. *A Short History of Drunkenness.* London: Penguin Random House, 2017
14. https://www.alcoholproblemsandsolutions.org/alcohol-in-the-middle-ages/
15. https://www.thedrinksbusiness.com/2016/10/1066-and-all-that-a-fateful-taste-for-ale/

Cate

1. https://www.workandincome.govt.nz/on-a-benefit/index.html
2. https://www.diabetes.org.uk/about_us/news/coronavirus

Tips for Moderating Your Drinking

1. https://simonsinek.com/find-your-why/
2. Nutt, David. *Drink? The New Science of Alcohol & Your Health.* London: Hodder & Stoughton Ltd, 2020

3. https://www.rethinkingdrinking.niaaa.nih.gov/
4. https://www.smartsheet.com/blog/essential-guide-writing-smart-goals
5. https://www.mindtools.com/pages/article/smart-goals.htm
6. Nutt, David. *Drink? The New Science of Alcohol & Your Health.* London: Hodder & Stoughton Ltd, 2020
7. https://www.rethinkingdrinking.niaaa.nih.gov/
8. https://www.drinkaware.co.uk/facts/health-effects-of-alcohol/mental-health/alcohol-withdrawal-symptoms
9. https://www.verywellmind.com/how-to-go-out-when-you-re-quitting-drinking-4788307
10. Gray, Catherine. *The Unexpected Joy of Being Sober.* London: Octopus Publishing Group Ltd, 2017
11. https://www.therecoveryvillage.com/family-friend-portal/excuses-addicts-denial/
12. https://www.benenden.co.uk/be-healthy/lifestyle/10-brilliant-things-to-do-instead-of-drinking-in-january/
13. 13.https://drinksint.com/news/fullstory.php/aid/9317/Alcoholic_drink_sales_soared_at_UK_supermarkets_over_Christmas.html
14. www.rethinkingdrinking.niaaa.nih.gov
15. https://www.youtube.com/watch?v=7EweM_ILVt4
16. https://www.nhs.uk/live-well/alcohol-support/tips-on-cutting-down-alcohol/

Units and Measures of Alcohol
1. https://www.nhs.uk/live-well/alcohol-support/calculating-alcohol-units/
2. https://www.gov.uk/weights-measures-and-packaging-the-law/specified-quantities

3. https://alcoholchange.org.uk/alcohol-facts/interactive-tools/check-your-drinking/alcohol-units
4. https://www.bbc.co.uk/news/health-21586566
5. https://www.omnicalculator.com/food/alcohol-by-volume#what-is-alcohol-by-volume
6. https://www.nhs.uk/live-well/alcohol-support/calculating-alcohol-units/
7. https://www.rethinkingdrinking.niaaa.nih.gov/how-much-is-too-much/what-counts-as-a-drink/whats-a-standard-drink.aspx
8. https://www.alcohol.org.nz/help-advice/standard-drinks/whats-a-standard-drink
9. https://alcoholthinkagain.com.au/alcohol-your-health/what-is-a-standard-drink/
10. https://alcoholchange.org.uk/alcohol-facts/interactive-tools/unit-calculator
11. https://www.nhs.uk/live-well/alcohol-support/binge-drinking-effects/
12. https://www.nhs.uk/live-well/alcohol-support/calculating-alcohol-units

Alcohol and Your Body

1. Nutt, David. *Drink? The New Science of Alcohol & Your Health.* London: Hodder & Stoughton Ltd, 2020
2. https://www.nhs.uk/live-well/eat-well/are-sweeteners-safe/
3. Nutt, David. *Drink? The New Science of Alcohol & Your Health.* London: Hodder & Stoughton Ltd, 2020
4. https://doclibrary-rcht.cornwall.nhs.uk/DocumentsLibrary/RoyalCornwallHospitals Trust/PatientInformation/General/RCHT1547Alcohol HowMuchIsTooMuch.pdf
5. https://pubmed.ncbi.nlm.nih.gov/23713737/

6. https://www.bhf.org.uk/informationsupport/heart-matters-magazine/medical/effects-of-alcohol-on-your-heart
7. https://www.ncbi.nlm.nih.gov/pmc/articles/PMC6804046/
8. http://www.colonic-association.org/blog/advice/booze-and-poos-what-alcohol-does-to-your-digestive-system/
9. https://www.medicalnewstoday.com/articles/326835
10. http://www.resourcesorg.co.uk/assets/pdfs/drinkingyouandyour.pdf
11. http://www.resourcesorg.co.uk/assets/pdfs/Alcohol%20&%20Reproduction.pdf
12. https://www.talktofrank.com/drug/cannabis?a=Marijuana
13. Elinore F. McCance-Katz et al. Concurrent cocaine-ethanol ingestion in humans: pharmacology, physiology, behavior, and the role of cocaethylene. Psychopharmacology volume 111, 1993
14. https://www.talktofrank.com/drug/ecstasy
15. https://www.talktofrank.com/drug/speed?a=Amphetamine
16. https://www.talktofrank.com/drug/heroin
17. https://www.sciencedirect.com/topics/pharmacology-toxicology-and-pharmaceutical-science/cathinone

Alcohol and Your Mind

1. https://www.bbc.co.uk/programmes/articles/558FD1c2hXHCh1wJfN6lkKS/how-wellness-became-big-business
2. https://www.who.int/news-room/fact-sheets/detail/mental-health-strengthening-our-response
3. https://alcoholchange.org.uk/alcohol-facts/fact-sheets/alcohol-statistics
4. https://www.ncbi.nlm.nih.gov/pmc/articles/PMC4493891/

5. https://www.ox.ac.uk/news/2017-01-06/your-health-benefits-social-drinking
6. https://camra.org.uk/
7. https://www.brookes.ac.uk/about-brookes/news/research-identifies-motivations-to-reduce-alcohol-intake/
8. https://alcoholchange.org.uk/alcohol-facts/fact-sheets/alcohol-and-mental-health
9. https://www.gov.uk/government/publications/prescribed-medicines-review-report/prescribed-medicines-review-summary
10. https://www.drinkaware.co.uk/facts/health-effects-of-alcohol/mental-health/alcohol-and-suicidal-thoughts

Some History of Alcohol in the United Kingdom

1. Forsyth, Mark. *A Short History of Drunkenness.* London: Penguin Random House, 2017
2. https://londonist.com/london/drink/gin-craze-history
3. Forsyth, Mark. *A Short History of Drunkenness.* London: Penguin Random House, 2017
4. https://www.historyhit.com/what-was-the-gin-craze-and-why-did-it-happen/
5. https://londonist.com/london/drink/gin-craze-history
6. Forsyth, Mark. *A Short History of Drunkenness.* London: Penguin Random House, 2017
7. https://www.historylearningsite.co.uk/stuart-england/william-iii/
8. https://londonist.com/2016/09/london-s-first-gin-boom
9. Forsyth, Mark. *A Short History of Drunkenness.* London: Penguin Random House, 2017
10. https://www.alcoholproblemsandsolutions.org/alcohol-in-the-18th-century-european-expansion/

11. Forsyth, Mark. *A Short History of Drunkenness.* London: Penguin Random House, 2017
12. https://theculturetrip.com/europe/united-kingdom/england/london/articles/why-is-london-dry-gin-called-that-and-how-is-it-made/
13. https://www.mentalfloss.com/article/62537/brief-history-tonic-water-your-gin-and-tonic
14. http://people.loyno.edu/~history/journal/1992-3/smith-r.htm
15. https://www.alcoholproblemsandsolutions.org/alcohol-in-the-19th-century/
16. http://www.branchcollective.org/?ps_articles=annemarie-mcallister-on-the-temperance-movement
17. https://www.bbc.co.uk/news/health-25712005
18. https://www.ncbi.nlm.nih.gov/books/NBK524982/
19. https://encyclopedia.1914-1918-online.net/article/drugs
20. ibid
21. ibid
22. https://blog.nationalarchives.gov.uk/pubs-vs-first-world-war/

The Marketing of Alcohol
1. https://www.allianceonline.co.uk/blog//2018/07/uk-licensing-laws-selling-alcohol-in-your-bar-or-restaurant/
2. https://www.gov.uk/weights-measures-and-packaging-the-law/specified-quantities
3. https://www.allianceonline.co.uk/blog//2018/07/uk-licensing-laws-selling-alcohol-in-your-bar-or-restaurant/
4. https://www.wordhippo.com/what-is/another-word-for/advertise.html

5. https://www.campaignmonitor.com/resources/knowledge-base/what-are-the-4-ps-of-marketing/
6. Nutt, David. *Drink? The New Science of Alcohol & Your Health.* London: Hodder & Stoughton Ltd, 2020
7. https://www.drivenmedia.co.uk/2020/01/17/a-potted-history-of-alcohol-advertising-and-that-self-driving-budweiser-truck/
8. https://www.carlsberg.com/en-gb
9. http://www.headington.org.uk/adverts/drinks_alcoholic.htm
10. https://www.statista.com/statistics/192158/us-ad-spending-of-anheuser-busch-inbev/https://www.verdict.co.uk/alcohol-brands-sports-sponsorship/
11. https://www.sportcal.com/
12. https://www.ns-businesshub.com/business/six-nations-2020-sponsors/
13. https://www.steinlager.com/
14. https://www.speights.co.nz/
15. https://www.ias.org.uk/alcohol_alert/issue-3-2002/#article-7
16. https://www.ias.org.uk/2019/10/16/its-time-to-call-time-on-the-use-of-gender-stereotypes-in-alcohol-marketing/
17. https://www.campaignlive.co.uk/article/under-16s-exposure-alcohol-ads-tv-drops-dramatically/1524492
18. https://search.proquest.com/openview/93485f693f153b5683e4d0a73ac170d2/1?pq-origsite=gscholar&cbl=48866
19. https://www.socialbakers.com/blog/alcohol-marketing-trends-you-need-to-know-right-now
20. Nicholls, James. *Every day, Everywhere: Alcohol Marketing and Social Media — Current Trends, Alcohol and Alcoholism*, Volume 47, Issue 4, July/August 2012, Pages 486-493, https://doi.org/10.1093/alcalc/ags043

21. https://www.drinkaware.co.uk/about-us/what-we-do
22. https://www.prweek.com/article/1493024/top-phe-adviser-quits-protest-its-choice-partner-new-responsible-drinking-campaign
23. Nutt, David. *Drink? The New Science of Alcohol & Your Health.* London: Hodder & Stoughton Ltd, 2020

The Impact of Alcohol

1. https://www.independent.co.uk/news/health/alcohol-booze-young-baby-boomers-generation-health-a9085771.html
2. https://www.ons.gov.uk/peoplepopulationandcommunity/healthandsocialcare/causesofdeath/bulletins/alcoholrelateddeathsintheunitedkingdom/registeredin2019
3. https://digital.nhs.uk/data-and-information/publications/statistical/statistics-on-alcohol/2020/part-1
4. https://www.theguardian.com/society/2019/jul/04/staggering-cost-nhs-alcohol-abuse-report
5. https://www.kcl.ac.uk/news/ten-percent-of-hospital-inpatients-are-alcohol-dependent
6. https://assets.publishing.service.gov.uk/government/uploads/system/uploads/attachment_data/file/864835/drink-drive-provisional-estimates-2018.pdf
7. https://njduidefense.lawyer/drunk-driving-statistics-worldwide/
8. https://iea.org.uk/wp-content/uploads/2016/07/DP_Alcohol%20and%20the%20public%20purse_63_amended2_web.pdf
9. https://www.who.int/violence_injury_prevention/violence/world_report/factsheets/fs_intimate.pdf
10. https://publichealthmatters.blog.gov.uk/2018/07/09/children-of-dependent-drinkers-your-innovation-fund-questions-answered/

11. https://www.bmgresearch.co.uk/much-alcohol-related-absence-costing-business/
12. https://academic.oup.com/occmed/article/71/2/62/6072139?login=true
13. https://www.bmj.com/content/366/bmj.l5274

The Alcohol Problem

1. Moscalewicz, J., and Vieczorek, L. (2017) Legal economies. The Role of The Alcohol Industry. Chapter 38 in Kolind, T., Thom, B. and Hunt, G. (eds) Handbook of Drug and Alcohol Studies Sage, London, pp 661-678.
2. https://www.who.int/substance_abuse/activities/gsrhua/en/
3. Moscalewicz, J., and Vieczorek, L. (2017) Legal economies. The Role of The Alcohol Industry. Chapter 38 in Kolind, T., Thom, B. and Hunt, G. (eds) Handbook of Drug and Alcohol Studies Sage, London, pp 661-678.
4. ibid
5. https://fingertips.phe.org.uk/profile/local-alcohol-profiles
6. https://assets.publishing.service.gov.uk/government/uploads/system/uploads/attachment_data/file/864835/drink-drive-provisional-estimates-2018.pdf
7. https://www.ons.gov.uk/peoplepopulationandcommunity/crimeandjustice/articles/thenatureofviolentcrimeinenglandandwales/yearendingmarch2018
8. https://fingertips.phe.org.uk/profile/local-alcohol-profiles
9. https://alcoholchange.org.uk/alcohol-facts/fact-sheets/alcohol-statistics
10. ibid

11. https://digital.nhs.uk/data-and-information/publications/statistical/health-survey-for-england/2018
12. http://allcatsrgrey.org.uk/wp/download/public_health/alcohol/24892-ALCOHOL-FRACTIONS-REPORT-A4-singles-24.3.14.pdf
13. https://www.who.int/bulletin/volumes/82/9/editorial20904html/en/

Is the Answer Prohibition?

1. https://www.britannica.com/event/Prohibition-United-States-history-1920-1933
2. https://www.theguardian.com/commentisfree/2020/jan/03/women-alcohol-drink-culture-prohibition-temperance
3. https://smileandgun.wordpress.com/2017/01/17/john-barleycorn-must-die-today-in-history-mock-funerals-took-place-across-america-as-prohibition-began/
4. https://www.history.com/news/10-things-you-should-know-about-prohibition
5. https://www.ncbi.nlm.nih.gov/pmc/articles/PMC1470475/
6. https://www.atlasobscura.com/articles/what-was-the-six-oclock-swill
7. http://www.factfiend.com/russia-used-received-40-state-income-selling-vodka/
8. https://inshorts.com/en/news/beer-was-considered-a-soft-drink-in-russia-until-2011-1489845443961
9. https://www.euro.who.int/en/health-topics/disease-prevention/alcohol-use/publications/2019/alcohol-policy-impact-case-study-the-effects-of-alcohol-control-measures-on-mortality-and-life-expectancy-in-the-russian-federation-2019
10. https://www.ncbi.nlm.nih.gov/pmc/articles/PMC7433289/

11. https://movendi.ngo/news/2020/05/13/alcohol-sales-ban-in-south-africa-benefits-and-big-alcohol-opposition/
12. https://ahauk.org/news/cmo-guidelines-still-missing-from-two-thirds-of-alcohol-labels/
13. https://assets.publishing.service.gov.uk/government/uploads/system/uploads/attachment_data/file/831562/PHE_Strategy_2020-25.pdf

Support Services and Treatments

1. Hanpatchaiyakul, K. Eriksson, H. Kijsompom, J. and Ostlund, G. (2016) Barriers to successful treatment of alcohol addiction as perceived by the healthcare professionals in Thailand - a Delphi study about obstacles and improvement suggestions. Glob Health Action (9) 31-38.
2. Kalema, D. Vanderplasschen, W. Vindevogel, S. Baguma, P. K. & Derluyn, I. (2017) Treatment challenges for alcohol service users in Kampala, Uganda. International Journal of alcohol and Drug research 6 (1) 27-35.
3. Flowers, W.D. Alcoholism/Drug Addiction A Disease or Not! iUniverse, Bloomington, New York. 2010
4. https://www.healthline.com/health/confabulation#:~:text=Confabulation%20is%20a%20symptom%20of,sound%20fantastical%20or%20made%20up
5. James O Prochaska, Carlo C DiClemente Psychotherapy: theory, research &practice. Division of Psychotherapy (29), American Psychological Association, (1982) 19: 3: 276.
6. J.O. Prochaska, CC DiClemente Journal of consulting and clinical psychology 51 (3), 390

Case Studies

1. Flowers, W.D. Alcoholism/Drug Addiction A Disease or Not! iUniverse, Bloomington, New York. 2010
2. ibid

About the Authors

Lesley Miller is a highly experienced and qualified ex-primary school teacher. Alongside 20 years teaching experience, she has extensive leadership experience and she holds the National Professional Qualification for Headship. Lesley has first-hand experience of the challenges of moderating or abstaining from alcohol and is keen to support others in realising that change is possible for everyone by finding a route that is suitable to them.

Cate Kell-Clarke is a New Zealand trained primary teacher with over 25 years of experience. She is trained in enquiry-based learning and has taught in New Zealand, Australia, Singapore and the United Kingdom. While teaching is her passion, eating, drinking and working in the hospitality trade have also played a large part in her life. Using her background in education, Cate is excited to offer support to those who wish to change their relationship with alcohol, as she has done.

Sylvain Tiecoura is an Alcohol & Drug Addiction Recovery Practitioner. He has worked with the NHS for many years and is currently employed as a substance misuse worker, working back in the community and supporting individuals and families to overcome their drug and alcohol addiction. He is skilled in Cognitive Behavioural Therapy (CBT), Social Services, Group Therapy, Clinical Research, and Crisis Intervention.

Appendix

Please note: This section of the book is copied directly from the NHS website as we did not feel comfortable in rewriting this extremely important information into our own words. Please check NHS website for further details

https://www.nhs.uk/conditions/alcohol-poisoning/

Alcohol poisoning: what to do

The signs and symptoms of alcohol poisoning include:

- Confusion
- Severely slurred speech
- Loss of co-ordination
- Vomiting
- Irregular or slow breathing
- Pale or blue-tinged skin caused by low body temperature (hypothermia)
- Being conscious but unresponsive (stupor)
- Passing out and being unconscious

In the most severe cases, alcohol poisoning can lead to coma, brain damage and death.

When to seek medical help:

If you suspect alcohol poisoning, dial 999 immediately to request an ambulance.

While you're waiting:

- Try to keep the person sitting up and awake
- Give them water if they can drink it
- If they have passed out, lie them on their side in the recovery position, and check that they're breathing properly
- Keep them warm
- Stay with them
- Never leave a person alone to 'sleep it off'.

The level of alcohol in a person's blood can continue to rise for up to 30 to 40 minutes after their last drink.

This can cause their symptoms to suddenly become much more severe. You also should not try to 'sober them up' by giving them coffee or putting them under a cold shower, for example. These methods will not help and may even be dangerous.

Books we found particularly helpful

- Forsyth, Mark. *A Short History of Drunkenness.* London: Penguin Random House, 2017
- Gray, Catherine. *The Unexpected Joy of Being Sober.* London: Octopus Publishing Group Ltd, 2017
- Hari, Johann. *Chasing the Scream.* London: Bloomsbury Publishing, 2019
- Nutt, David. *Drink? The New Science of Alcohol & Your Health.* London: Hodder & Stoughton Ltd, 2020

Further Help and Support

Alcohol Change: www.alcoholchange.org.uk

Alcoholics Anonymous: www.alcoholics-anonymous.org.uk

Drinkaware: www.drinkaware.co.uk/advice/support-services/alcohol-support-services

Drug Addiction: Getting help: www.nhs.uk/live-well/healthy-body/drug-addiction-getting-help/

Samaritans: www.samaritans.org

Treatment for Alcohol Problems: www.niaaa.nih.gov

Index

A
abstinence 8, 10, 15, 17, 23, 36, 60, 71, 104, 105, 128, 129, 149, 157, 168
accidents 82, 131, 132, 138
addiction 9, 15, 23, 27, 31, 32, 33, 83, 152, 154, 155, 156, 157, 162, 183, 185, 188
advertising 116, 117, 119, 120, 121, 123, 124, 127, 143, 145, 165, 179
Advertising Standards Authority 123
alcohol by volume 74
alcohol poisoning 79, 186
amphetamines 96, 97
Ancient China 35
Ancient civilization 34
Ancient Egypt 36, 37
Ancient Greece 38
Anxiety 104
Australia 12, 50, 53, 54, 75, 76, 132, 143, 185

B
baby boomers 129
body systems 90
boredom 54, 65, 86

C
Campaign for Real Ale, CAMRA 102
children 27, 53, 54, 56, 80, 81, 85, 106, 109, 123, 124, 133, 134, 144, 160, 161, 162, 163, 180
circulatory system 91
cocaine 26, 28, 95, 160, 176
Cycle of Change 102, 155

D
Department for Work and Pensions (DWP) 6
depressants 27, 97
depression 12, 26, 39, 91, 102, 103, 104, 114, 132, 135, 142
digestive system 92, 93
domestic abuse 132, 133, 135
Domestic Purposes Benefit 47
dopamine 30, 95
Dutch Courage 50, 107, 113

E
eat well 69
ecstasy (MDMA) 28, 96
education 1, 2, 7, 10, 59, 85, 126, 127, 147, 149, 185
emotional wellbeing 99
endorphins 30
exercise 68, 99

F
First World War 113, 141

G
gamma-aminobutyric acid 29
generation 22, 128, 129, 180
genetics 32
glutamate 29

H
hallucinogens 28
health advisor 89
healthy alternatives 68
heroin 26, 27, 28, 97, 176

L
legal highs 28, 97
London Dry gins 110
lost income 134

M
marijuana (cannabis) 95
marketing 22, 87, 90, 98, 115, 116, 118, 121, 124, 125, 126, 139, 143, 179
mental health 8, 19, 32, 55, 56, 85, 91, 98, 99, 101, 102, 103, 133, 135, 152, 159, 168
millennials 128
minimum pricing 129, 135, 136, 144, 145
moderate 7, 15, 30, 38, 60, 65, 77, 82, 103, 105, 111, 112, 113, 126, 134, 145, 170
Moderation 1, 2, 8, 10, 15, 23, 36, 59, 71, 100, 105, 111, 128, 149
Mother's Ruin 108, 109

N
negatives 62
nervous system 29, 77, 91, 97
neuromodulators 30
New Zealand 12, 42, 43, 45, 46, 47, 48, 50, 53, 75, 76, 116, 121, 143, 185
NHS 12, 72, 79, 86, 89, 93, 130, 131, 132, 138, 185, 186
nicotine 28, 94
non-alcoholic alternatives 170
No Treating Order 113
Novel Psychoactive Substances (NPS) 28

O
opiates 28
opioids 28

P
peer pressure 32, 66
positives 62, 166
prehistoric man 33
prohibition 11, 26, 34, 136, 140, 141, 142, 143, 144, 145, 146, 147, 148, 182

Q
quinine 110

R
reducing 62, 72, 100, 129, 139

reproductive system 94
rewards 69
road traffic accidents 82, 132
Russia 144, 145

S
Scotland 107, 135, 145
SMART goals 63
social media 8, 17, 22, 98, 116, 124, 125, 126
South Africa 132, 145, 146
sponsorship 121, 179
stimulants 28
sugar cravings 65
Support Services and Treatments 4, 149, 183

T
Teetotal Movement 110, 111
Temperance Movement 111, 119, 143
The Dark Ages 40
The Roman Empire 39, 40
The Six O'Clock Swill 143
triggers 42, 100, 161

U
units 16, 29, 64, 72, 73, 74, 75, 76, 77, 78, 79, 80, 82, 88, 89, 92, 100, 129, 138, 145, 152, 159, 174, 175
Universal Credit 6

W
withdrawal symptoms 65, 82, 156
World Health Organisation 98, 137, 139, 145

www.ingramcontent.com/pod-product-compliance
Lightning Source LLC
Chambersburg PA
CBHW071733080526
44588CB00013B/2007